GWENDOLYN BROOKS
AND
WORKING WRITERS

GWENDOLYN BROOKS

AND

WORKING WRITERS

edited by
Jacqueline Imani Bryant

THIRD WORLD PRESS
Chicago

Third World Press
Publishers since 1967

First Edition
Printed in the United States of America
Cover, inside text layout and design by Relana Johnson

Library of Congress Cataloging-in-Publication Data

Gwendolyn Brooks and working writers / edited by Jacqueline Imani Bryant.
    p. cm.
  Includes bibliographical references.
  ISBN 978-0-88378-279-8 (alk. paper)
 1. Brooks, Gwendolyn, 1917-2000–Influence. I. Bryant, Jacqueline I.
II. Brooks, Gwendolyn, 1917-2000.
  PS3503.R7244Z6595 2007
  811'.54–dc22
                                    2007010393

12 11 10 09 08 07   8 7 6 5 4 3 2 1

Grateful acknowledgements for the use of photographs are given to Margaret T.
Burroughs, Joanne V. Gabbin, Quraysh Ali Lansana, Gwendolyn Brooks
Permissions and Third World Press archives.

CONTENTS

PART TWO
THE MOTHER, FRIEND

PART THREE
THE TEACHER

ACKNOWLEDGEMENTS

I thank Gwendolyn Brooks for being. I thank her for transforming lives and landscapes with her person and her pen.

I thank Haki R. Madhubuti for this brilliant idea, "Gwendolyn Brooks and Working Writers." Each writer shares a different experience. Each experience reflects the same theme– the sustained influence and enduring quality of Gwendolyn Brooks' works and life. I thank him for his ongoing encouragement and support over the years. I also thank his ready, capable, and friendly staff at Third World Press.

I give special thanks to Gwendolyn Brooks' daughter, Nora Brooks Blakely, for showcasing her talent and inspiring audiences while directing her Chocolate Chips Theatre production, "A Day in Bronzeville: Black Life Through The Eyes of Gwendolyn Brooks" (2005). The power of the poet's words still resonates.

To the writers who took the time to excavate, inscribe, and share the experience, I cannot thank you enough. Your collective voice demonstrates the generative power of the word and the significant role the writer plays in literally transforming lives.

To my colleagues and students, who remain supportive, I thank you. For technical assistance, I thank my niece, Robin Johnson, and her colleague, Aaron Roth.

To each member of my immediate and extended family, my parents, Mr. James C. Peterson and Mrs. Alberta B. Peterson, my husband, Louis, my loving daughter, Angela, and my sister, Beverly Johnson, I sincerely appreciate your ongoing support.

INTRODUCTION
GWENDOLYN BROOKS, THE GIVER

Gwendolyn Brooks and Working Writers offers a glimpse of the influence Gwendolyn Brooks had and has on the lives and works of writers. The following representative voices proclaim the enduring quality of her work, the indelible mark of her presence, and the indefatigable work of her Spirit. Gwendolyn Brooks literally dispensed time, patience, and kindness. Each writer acknowledges this while reflecting on varied experiences. Time, place, and participants differ; yet, each narrative proclaims the vitality of the word and the power of the human spirit. Both endure. Both affect change.

I witnessed such a change after taking Cleveland State University students to Chicago State for the Sixth Annual Gwendolyn Brooks Conference in 1996. The students experienced Gwendolyn Brooks' presence, heard her voice, and absorbed her feedback on their creative works. They were transformed. Rather than engage in idle chit chat, the students crafted and critiqued poems as we drove back to Cleveland. In essence, they workshopped en route. During the days following our return to Cleveland, their enthusiasm heightened rather than diminished. Because Cleveland State University provided travel funds for the conference, students were required to share their experiences in a public university forum. They did so willingly and emotionally. Following the public forum, the Director of Black Studies, Dr. Howard A. Mims, observing heightened enthusiasm and unharnessed emotion, invited the students to share their experiences with the wider Cleveland audience on his weekly radio show. Clearly, the patient presence and precise words of Gwendolyn

Brooks empowered and transformed these students who, in turn, altered the environment in which they studied, worked, and lived.

Living in Chicago a few years later, I was honored to be a faculty member in the department with Distinguished Professor of English Gwendolyn Brooks. I took advantage of every opportunity to hear her speak. One such opportunity occurred on October 9, 2000 when she served as the guest speaker in the Gwendolyn Brooks Seminar. I often recall Gwendolyn Brooks' participating in this Gwendolyn Brooks Seminar held in the Gwendolyn Brooks Center at Chicago State University. As I contemplate how this internationally-known poet and novelist critiqued her novel, *Maud Martha*, with the enthusiasm of the seminar participants, I cherish that moment more knowing now that even while ill, Gwendolyn Brooks gave of herself and her talent. She embodied the command, "Conduct your blooming in the noise and whip of the whirlwind" (Blacks 456). This activity of giving, "in spite of," is a persistent theme, not only in the entries that follow but in numerous other published works.

Embedded in scholarly works, creative works, newspaper articles, and magazine articles, one hears the writer's voice extolling the influence of Gwendolyn Brooks' life and works. For example, Lerone Bennett, Jr., noted historian and executive director of *Ebony*, and family friend, stated shortly after Gwendolyn Brooks' transition that

> she was one of the great poets and spirits of our time . . . She was a giant of American literature and a major force for African American writers and all other writers and poets. She was a major influence on the writers' movement of the '60s, '70s, and '80s, and she has generously mentored hundreds, possibly thousands of

poets with her own money and resources. (52)
Bennett recalls spirit, force, influence, and generosity. With these powerful sources permeating her life and works, Gwendolyn Brooks redirected lives and redesigned literary landscapes. Her voice would serve as yet another powerful source. Journalist Mary Schmich shares two lessons learned from the life and works of Gwendolyn Brooks: "Show your neck. Free your voice." According to Schmich, Brooks links the exposed neckline and the clear voice. Brooks observed that especially young women "'spoke not from the gut and the heart but from some traffic jam in their throats. They needed to reach down through that constriction,' she said, 'and pull their voice up from somewhere deep and true'" (1). It is Gwendolyn Brooks' ever present voice hovering over the print and stored in aural memory that endures.

Listen to the individual writer's voice: Maggie Anderson, Molefi Kete Asante, Regina Harris Baiocchi, Margaret G. T. Burroughs, Joanne V. Gabbin, Sam Greenlee, Quraysh Ali Lansana, Paule Marshall, D. H. Melhem, Gwendolyn A. Mitchell, Georgene Bess Montgomery, Adele Newson-Horst, Mwatabu S. Okantah, Useni Eugene Perkins, L. E. Scott, Dorothy Randall Tsuruta, and Shirley N. Weber. Each recalls the world renowned Poet/Mother/Friend, and Teacher, the chosen place, the memorable poem, and/or the generative power of the word. Each illuminates Gwendolyn Brooks' indomitable spirit of giving, a viable force that contributes to the eternal influence of her life and works.

Jacqueline Imani Bryant

Works Cited

Bennett, Lerone Jr. "Gwendolyn Brooks, 83, Who Won Pulitzer Prize For *Poetry, Dies*." Jet Magazine. Dec. 2000: 52.

Brooks, Gwendolyn. *Blacks*. Chicago: Third World Press, 1994.

Schmich, Mary. "Brooks Gave Strength to Others through her Voice." *Chicago Tribune*. 6 Dec. 2000, sec. 2: 1

XI
One Wants a Teller in a Time like This

One wants a Teller in a time like this.

One's not a man, one's not a woman grown,
To bear enormous business all alone.

One cannot walk this winding street with pride,
Straight-shouldered, tranquil-eyed,
Knowing one knows for sure the way back home.
One wonders if one has a home.

One is not certain if or why or how.
One wants a Teller now:–

Put on your rubbers and you won't catch cold.
Here's hell, there's heaven. Go to Sunday School.
Be patient, time brings all good things–(and cool
Strong balm to the burning at the brain?)–
Behold,
Love's true, and triumphs; and God's actual.

Gwendolyn Brooks
from *Annie Allen*, "The Womanhood"

PART ONE

THE POET

"Home and library taught me that books are the bandages and voyages. Links to light. Keys and hammers. Ripe redeemers. Dials and bells and healing hallelujah."

–Gwendolyn Brooks
from *Report From Part Two*

THOUGHTS ON GWENDOLYN BROOKS

Sam Greenlee

In my multiple roles of poet, novelist, screenwriter, producer, director, actor, professor, and former track star, I did not meet Gwendolyn Brooks until the late 1960s. Some time later, I was honored to receive a Gwendolyn Brooks Award for Poetry.

In response to the statement, "Explain how Gwendolyn Brooks' works and life experiences have influenced your work and/or life as a writer," I would say, just knowing Gwendolyn Brooks was an experience. She was beautiful and attractive because of her intelligence. Gwendolyn Brooks also possessed a sense of humor and wit.

Regarding Gwendolyn Brooks' style, I observe the influences of e.e. cummings and Langston Hughes in her earlier works. Gwendolyn Brooks not only utilized but transformed European elements in her poetry. African American art forms are eclectic. We have historically borrowed and then created something of our own. Musicality is another identifiable feature of Gwendolyn Brooks' works. Her poems are suitable for the blues, church hymns, etc. Gwendolyn Brooks bridged writers of the 1930s and 1940s, and the 1950s and 1960s. I see no division between her earlier and later works. She evolved over time. Unfortunately, many young women poets today have not read the works of Gwendolyn Brooks; their works reveal this.

Because I was out of the country for several years, I last interacted with Gwendolyn Brooks during the mid 1990s. Gwendolyn Brooks and I happened to be on the same train traveling back to Chicago from the East coast. I returned to the U.S. in June 2000. Gwendolyn Brooks made her transition December 3, 2000. God cries when the good ones go.

To be true to Gwendolyn Brooks and her works, we must read her poetry and produce it on stage. All Chicago State University (CSU) students should complete a Gwendolyn Brooks Seminar as a graduation requirement. No student should leave CSU without knowing about the life and works of former Poet Laureate of Illinois, first Black Pulitzer Prize winner of poetry, and Distinguished Professor of English Gwendolyn Brooks. In fact, Chicago State University should be named "GWENDOLYN BROOKS UNIVERSITY."

Unlike many writers who hide behind their works, Gwendolyn Brooks is in her works. Because she did not hide behind her works, Gwendolyn Brooks became a great writer. "Unpretentiously real, she works her crown with the casual ease of a Baptist sister on her way to church."

[Interviewed by Jacqueline Imani Bryant.]

GWENDOLYN BROOKS, FRIEND AND MENTOR

D. H. MELHEM

For a writer, who must develop the stamina of a long distance runner through miles, years, and often a lifetime of disappointment and rejection, self-confidence is a basic part of the psychic travel kit. Early recognition, by parents, teachers, and the world, instilled that confidence in Gwendolyn Brooks. The first two elements also supported me. As for the world, it withheld acceptance until much later. Even so, other parallels and similarities between us eased our communication and mutual regard as friends. They also facilitated that somewhat ambiguous yet catalytic entity called "influence."

In a sense, Gwendolyn Brooks spoke to me long before we met. I already had some slight though favorable knowledge of her work. I liked it for its humanity and closeness to everyday life. Our relationship began in a real place and time: the City College of New York, 1971. I had just completed my master's thesis on the poetics of Charles Olson when I learned that Brooks was coming to the college in the fall as a Distinguished Professor of the Arts. I immediately applied for admission to her class. But I was now a doctoral student at the CUNY Graduate Center and could not enroll in her master's level class for credit. Nevertheless, after submitting poems (which would appear in my first book, *Notes on 94th Street*), I was thrilled to be warmly accepted by Brooks as an auditor. In person, we were compatible from the very beginning. I was writing about my neighborhood just as she had done in *A Street in Bronzeville*. In fact, it could almost be said that Brooks's first book, with its mixture of local and national subjects, unconsciously served as a template for mine.

Brooks and I met as mature women. The Feminist Movement was reverberating in the stresses of our longtime marriages. We were both mothers of a son and a daughter. As writers we were chronic revisers. We believed that poetry could be a social act of spiritual and political engagement. And we were both teachers. I had taught my first class (substituting for an ailing English professor at City) while attending Brooks's workshop as a student.

I loved her classroom presence—alive with politics as well as poetry, and it influenced my own classroom style. Once in her workshop we debated whether "A poem should not mean / but be," lines from "Ars Poetica" by Archibald MacLeish, who had served as a Consultant in Poetry to the Library of Congress. With typical generosity, she once told me that I "helped her teach the class." We became friends.

Brooks was a delightful companion. Despite her seriousness, she had a positive yet wryly comic view of life, glimpsed in her work. I accompanied her on shopping trips; I was present at nearly all her readings and appearances in New York City, although sometimes she preferred to slip quietly into town. We dined together (at her insistence, I was usually a guest), and we both enjoyed good food and conversation. When we spoke on the telephone, the first topic was always Family, and the first family to be discussed was always mine. She was expressing her values, her regard for others, by example. Her regard for "the Black Family" extended her personal concerns.

As a teacher, Brooks was supportive of her students' poetry. She understood how publication helped to build a writer's confidence. In her class we compiled a little anthology, called *Twelve and a Half* (as auditor, I was the "half"). She knew how much early publishing had fortified her—*A Street in Bronzeville* was published to a warm critical reception when she was 28 years old. She encouraged me, in my middle age, to have my first book published and gave me a commendation for its cover. When she was invited to serve on the Pulitzer Prize Committee, she proposed my *Notes on 94th Street* (1972) for a nomination. Though it was not forthcoming, her affirmation, plus the excitement of hope, meant everything to me.

Brooks showed me how one could grow and change throughout life. At 50, she moved away from supporting integration to advocating Black Nationalism. In mid-career, despite her early success with rhyme and conventional form, which she modified, nevertheless, as in "The Anniad" in *Annie Allen* (1949), for which she was "Pulitzerized," as she put it, she moved toward free verse. Instead of capitalizing the beginning of each line, she capitalized only where the verse began a sentence. Turning away from the sonnet, she felt she was responding to the times and their evolving needs.

Brooks was a deeply loyal person. She had absorbed the precepts of her "Duty-Loving" mother, Keziah Wims Brooks, as I had absorbed the admonitions of my own father, who combined idealism with a sense of the morally "proper" or "important" thing to do. Brooks approved of my taking care of my husband after his stroke, even though he and I had been divorced. In her own life, she nursed her husband through illness (and her mother, as well), even when the couple conducted separate lives while sharing the same roof—shelter the poet willingly provided. On a less profound level, we were both reared with a respect for middle-class courtesies, amenities of social behavior that seem to be submerged (if not drowned) in our "casual" society. She answered all her voluminous correspondence, sent thank you notes, expressed appreciation. As she was fond of remarking, "My religion is kindness."

Like my own mother, who died prematurely and extended me an oceanic affection and affirmation, people we love abide within us. Regarding Gwendolyn Brooks, we enjoy the further bounty of her magnificent poetry. When I wrote her a poem, she honored me by offering a title change, from "For Gwendolyn Brooks" to, simply, "Gwendolyn Brooks." Its first section expresses what I admired in her and her work, and continue to emulate as best I can.

Gwendolyn Brooks

A matter of poetry and power: the power of
poetry raised to the rhetoric of
music, an orchestration by cultural strings, chords
of drums and chanting
toward harmony or dissonance
a syncopation of
rage and rejoicing
an architecture
familial
      the strength is love
      soled and sewn, the
      underside of anger like
      sun, its ray sustaining the eye
      lifting to the face of a child
      with its day ahead

                  D. H. Melhem

FROM "SATIN-LEGS" TO A SATIN TOUCH: FOR GWENDOLYN BROOKS

Mwatabu S. Okantah

It scares me to death to realize
that if I hadn't lived beyond the age
of 50, I would have never have come
to properly appreciate my blackness.
　　　　　　　　–Gwendolyn Brooks

　　so
　　down to
　　earth;
　　grew from *straight*
　　to *natural*—
　　no more
　　negro-fraction are you.
　　gentle
　　woman poet.
　　Third Sermon on the Warpland
　　poet in righteous black.
　　you poem'd soft-
　　hard
　　black-life thoughts
　　that celebrated Lincoln West
　　lives in metered
　　revolution…

10

I will always remember my first experience hearing Gwendolyn Brooks "read" her poetry. I was a 23-year-old student who wanted to be a poet. Miss Brooks was the featured poet at the Tenth Anniversary Celebration of Dudley Randall's Broadside Press. I was stunned by her originality. She soared above the limiting constraints of a mere poetry reading. After hearing Sonia Sanchez, Haki Madhubuti, Mari Evans and Etheridge Knight, I literally became intoxicated by the sounds of Black poets performing their own words. I had been thrown into new language space; somewhere in between ordinary speech and talking in tongues. For the first real time, I was encountering the natural music inside Black poetry.

I learned to listen for the *word sounds* I hear singing in my inner ear. During her workshop at that 1975 Broadside gathering, Miss Brooks stressed the need for young writers to develop a healthy respect for the writing process. She stressed the importance of craft. She directed us to read, and find our own voice in relation to the full range of voices to be found in the great Black tradition in poetry. She echoed sentiments she articulated in Broadside's *A Capsule Course in Black Poetry Writing* (Brooks, Kgositsile, Madhubuti, Randall):

> 1966. 1967. 1968. Years of explosion. In those years a young black with with pen in hand responded not to pretty sunsets and the lapping of lake water but to the speech of physical riot and spiritual rebellion. Young blacks went to see "The Battle of Algiers" rather than the latest Rock Hudson movie. Young blacks stopped saluting Shakespeare, A. E. Housman, T. S. Eliot. They began to shake hands with Franz Fanon, Malcolm X—gulping down the now "classic" *The Wretched of the Earth*, the *Autobiography* and

Message to the Grass Roots. And after such seeing,
after such gulping, there had to be a Difference. There
had to be hard reckonings…. There were things to be
said to black brothers and sisters and these things—
annunciatory, curative, inspiriting—were to be
said forthwith, without frill, and without fear of the
white presence. [1]

Miss Brooks became a primary influence in my development as a writer when I needed it most. Looking back, I now realize she recognized something in me I did not see in myself.

I was brought to that conference against my will by the late Hulda Smith-Graham, one of my college writing instructors who became my cultural midwife. As we all gathered closely around Miss Brooks that day, she gently coaxed me to read in spite of my reluctance. She could hear Hulda urging me to read. I tried mightily to ignore her, but Gwendolyn deftly stepped in and pulled me out of my poetic closet. I can only imagine the countless number of now no-longer-young writers she touched in similar fashion. I also suspect that all of us remember being astounded that Gwendolyn Brooks had acknowledged our creative existence. She seemed to always offer a kind word and encouragement for your work. For the first time in my life, I was willing to take myself seriously as a poet because Gwendolyn Brooks had taken me seriously. And, over the next twenty or more years, she never changed in that regard. She always remembered me no matter how much time passed between meetings.

I had become "caught up" in a general feeling—it seemed to be in the air—that was also erupting inside of me. Black Godmother poet Gwendolyn sounded a voice of wisdom and reason. Writing in her insightful piece, "The Field of the Fever, the Time of the Tall-Walkers," from her 1972 autobiography *Report from Part One*, she captured her feelings attending the Fisk University Writers' Conference in the spring of 1967: "Until 1967 my own Blackness did not confront me with a shrill spelling of itself. I knew that I was what most people were calling 'a Negro'; I called myself that, although always the word fell awkwardly on a poet's ear; I had never liked the sound of it …"[2] By 1972, I was encouraged by her honesty. Gwendolyn was an Elder who joined us. Negro? Colored? Nigger? I felt her words at a time in my life when I, too, was groping in search of our proper name. She also added the following observation:

> Suddenly there was New Black to meet.…I was aware
> of a general energy, an electricity, in look, walk, speech,
> *gesture* of the young Blackness I saw all about me. I
> had been 'loved' at South Dakota State College. Here,
> I was coldly Respected. Here, the heroes included the
> novelist-director John Killens, editors David Llorens
> and Hoyt Fuller, playwright Ron Milner, historians
> John Henrik Clarke and Lerone Bennett (and even
> poor Lerone was taken to task, by irate members of a
> no-nonsense young audience, for affiliating himself
> with *Ebony Magazine*, considered at that time a traitor
> for allowing skin-bleach advertisements in its pages,
> and for over-featuring light-skinned women).[3]

Gwendolyn reminded me of my mother's eldest sister—my Aunt Hattie, all quiet and serene yet strong-voiced. At a time when so many of our Elders dismissed us as having lost our natural minds, she wrote: "I—who have 'gone the gamut' from an almost angry rejection of my dark skin by some of my brainwashed brothers and sisters to a surprised queenhood in the new Black sun—am qualified to enter at least the kindergarten of new consciousness now….I have hopes for myself."[4] I was forever guided onto the right aesthetic path when she added,

> I know now that I am essentially an essential African, in occupancy here because of an indeed 'peculiar' institution….I know now that Black Fellow-feeling must be the Black man's encyclopedic Primer….I know that the Black-and-white integration concept, which in the mind of some beaming early saint was a dainty spinning dream, has wound down to farce, to unsavory and mumbling farce…[5]

I look back on those heady times from the perspective of now being in *my* 50s, and I am thankful I was blessed to *experience* her Black satin poet's presence. Gwendolyn Brooks touched into so many of our lives. I truly believe that from the House of the Ancestors, she will have an even greater impact. She will touch into even more peoples' lives because we poets will continue to invoke her guardian Angel Spirit. We will continue to call her name. Godmother Gwendolyn always knew there is a little Lincoln West in all of us still. And, like Lincoln,

> When he was hurt, too much
> stared at—
> too much
> left alone—he
> thought about that. He told himself
> "After all, I'm
> the real thing."
>
> It comforted him.[6]

Endnotes

1. Gwendolyn Brooks. "Gwendolyn Brooks." *A Capsule Course in Black Poetry Writing*. Detroit: Broadside Press, 1975. 3-4.
2. Gwendolyn Brooks. "The Field of the Fever, the Time of the Tall-Walkers." *Black Women Writers (1950-1980): A Critical Evaluation*. Ed. Mari Evans. Garden City: Anchor Press/Doubleday, 1984. 75.
3. Brooks, 76.
4. Brooks, 77.
5. Brooks, 77-78.
6. Gwendolyn Brooks, ed. *A Broadside Treasury: 1965-1970*. Detroit: Broadside Press, 1971. 36.

MEMORIES OF
GWENDOLYN BROOKS
Useni Eugene Perkins

Although I was not one of Gwendolyn Brooks' personal friends or a member of the group of writers that she shepherded, I always felt a close kinship with her. No doubt this feeling emanated from my informal contacts with her, her relationship with my deceased parents, and her genuine concern for Black writers. I cannot recall the first time I met Ms. Brooks, but it was most likely during the early forties at the South Side Art Center, which had emerged as a major cultural institution for Black artists in the wake of the ill-fated depression of the thirties.

A product of President Franklin Delano Roosevelt's WPA program, the South Side Art Center attracted many seasoned and fledgling Black artists who sought to hone their respective crafts in an environment sensitive to their creative spirits. Among these artists were Charles White, Margaret Burroughs, Bernard Goss, Archibald Motley, Margaret Danner, Frank Marshall Davis, and my father, Marion

Perkins. Also, on occasions, such notables as Paul Robeson and Langston Hughes would visit this historic institution.

If my memory serves me correctly, I believe that Ms. Brooks was a secretary at the Center during the formative stage of her distinguished career. As a youth, I visited the South Side Art Center (located a few blocks from my birthplace) many times, primarily because my father was one of its principal supporters. Again, if my memory serves me correctly, I attended one of several receptions held at the Center in honor of Ms. Brooks after she won the prestigious Pulitzer Prize in 1950 for her volume of poetry, *Annie Allen* (1949).

Later, when I attended Wendell Phillips High School, I would occasionally see Ms. Brooks at various cultural gatherings when I accompanied my parents. These gatherings were generally held in Hyde Park at the home of Ed and Joyce Gourfain, strong supporters of Black artists. At these gatherings, one would meet artists like the legendary blues singer Big Bill Broonzy, Oscar Brown, Jr., Studs Terkel, Etta Moten Barnett, and, of course, Gwendolyn Brooks and her husband, Henry Blakely.

My interest in poetry began when I was in the sixth grade, although at the time I had not read any of Ms. Brooks' works. Langston Hughes was my major influence, and it was not until I had finished high school that I began to have an interest in Ms. Brooks' poetry. As my interest in her work resonated, I began to appreciate her lyrical use of words and how she was able to paint a picture of everyday people with whom I could identify. Also, because many of her poems portrayed scenes in Bronzeville, where I lived, I had a greater appreciation of them.

During the sixties, I appeared on several programs with Ms. Brooks and was always impressed with her humility and professional demeanor. This was, indeed, an exciting period in Chicago's expanding Black Arts Movement, and Ms. Brooks was becoming an inspiration to many young poets. Her association with poets like Haki Madhubuti, Carolyn Rogers, Walter Bradford, Angela Jackson, Sterling Plumpp, and others made her a much sought after and respected literary icon.

Finally, my greatest affection for Ms. Brooks stems from her unprecedented support of young writers and her nurturing spirit to help children realize their creative potential. During her tenure as Poet Laureate of Illinois, she generously gave financial and moral support to many aspiring writers and also to those who had achieved some recognition.

As I look back over the years, I can honestly say that it was a privilege to have been in the presence of this most remarkable, talented, and humble lady while she graced us with her life-affirming poetry and indomitable spirit.

GEORGIA – NEW JERSEY – VIETNAM – GWENDOLYN BROOKS: REFLECTIONS

L. E. Scott

Georgia

On September 7, 1947 I was born on "Mr. Hays' farm" in Arabi, Georgia, the last child in a family of fifteen–eight girls and seven boys. Our father, like his father and his father (who had been "freed" by Abraham Lincoln), was a sharecropper and our mother, like her mother and her mother (who had been "freed" by Abraham Lincoln), was a sharecropper's wife. By all accounts, "Mr. Hays" was "a good white man for his day." My father worked "Mr. Hays' farm" for years and so did his wife and children. Every year "Mr. Hays" told my father that the farm had made no money (he showed my father all the paperwork–my father could neither read nor write), and my father got further and further into debt to this "good white man." By the time we ran away from "Mr. Hays' farm" in the middle of the night, life had hurt my father, as it had so many other Black men of his time. My father never healed.

New Jersey

We headed North to Trenton, New Jersey, where I was enrolled in my first "real" school. It had brick buildings and a different teacher for each subject. Not only that, it was "integrated." I was in a world I didn't know. To the northern Black students I was "country." As for the white students, my first 13 years had taught me their kind called me "nigger" as if it was a birthmark and as if it was their birthright to do so. Northern racism just wore a different smile.

In school, I lived in my head and I started to write.

Vietnam

In March 1967, less than a year after graduating from high school, I was drafted into the Army. My father had served in World War One and the armed forces had been my older brothers' escape route from "Mr. Hays' farm," so when I received my draft notice, no one in my family said, "Don't go." It was at Fort Jackson during my combat training that one of the young Black recruits began talking to the other Brothers about refusing to go to Vietnam to fight in this unjust war being waged by the white man on a People of Color. At the time, I didn't understand what he was trying to teach us. I had seen what America had done to my father, but at 19, I didn't hate America, and I didn't understand how much hate she had for me. But I would learn.

In September 1967, I was flown to Vietnam and while I was out on "search-and-destroy" missions for America, the cities of my country were catching fire with the cries of "Freedom Now! Justice Now!" Black Americans were dying on the streets. Then it happened. Eight months and two Purple Hearts into my time in Vietnam, Dr. Martin Luther King, Jr. was assassinated by an evil that was eating well in the country of my birth. America had done enough to me now!

Gwendolyn Brooks

When I arrived in Chicago in June 1971, I was a damaged man with a handful of poems. Some of the poems were about Georgia, some were about New Jersey, and some were about Vietnam. I was in Chicago for the International Black Writers' Conference (the founder/director of which was the late Mrs. Alice Browning). A friend had told me that the famous poet, Ms. Gwendolyn Brooks, would be there and that she conducted workshops to help young writers.

As I look back now on that first meeting with Ms. Brooks, I realize that somehow she knew I was hurting. She spoke to me and with me, and by the time I left Chicago I had given her my handful of poems. Some weeks later I received a note from her. She had taken the time to write some encouraging words about my poems, and I wrapped those words around me with joy.

I attended that conference each year until 1973, and if Ms. Brooks was in town, she would come by. It was always enriching to be in her presence. During those years, I would send her poems from time to time, to which she responded with kind and helpful words.

In September 1974, I left the United States of America to travel and live in Africa and other parts of the world. Whenever I had a book of poems published, I would send a copy to Ms. Brooks–and she in turn would send me copies of her books.

In the 1980s, I spent some time working with Aborigine writers in Australia and Maori writers in Aotearoa/New Zealand. In the course of that work, I wrote to Ms. Brooks and told her that the indigenous writers of these two countries found her work powerful and wanted to know more about her and other African American writers. I informed her that I was editing an anthology of African American writers (entitled *Each Other's Dreams*) and that I hoped she would allow me to use some of her poems. Ms. Brooks consented and sent not only her poems but also her love to the Brothers and Sisters in this part of the world. The Aborigine and Maori people felt a special kinship to Ms. Brooks and the other African American writers who shared their words with them.

When I think of Ms. Gwendolyn Brooks, I think not just of her literary legacy but also of a day in June 1971 when her insightfulness, kindness, and love for her people touched my wounds, and how her words of encouragement over the years helped a young Black man from Georgia learn the power of the WORD!

HOMAGE TO GWENDOLYN BROOKS, OUR PRIDE AND JOY

Dorothy Randall Tsuruta

Each semester that I teach my survey of African American literature course, among the poems always included is Gwendolyn Brooks' "To An Old Black Woman, Homeless and Indistinct." We who read and appreciate Brooks' poetry, and in turn are inspired by her, all have our very own favorites. The same is true of the vignettes in her one novel, *Maud Martha*. One of the most personally moving literary experiences I have had in recent years was the occasion to sequester off with *Maud Martha*, rereading it, thinking about it, and writing about it in the essay that ultimately was included in *Gwendolyn Brooks' Maud Martha: A Critical Collection*, edited by Jacqueline Bryant.

Black literature, as I lecture ceaselessly and wholeheartedly to my students at San Francisco State University, is "Art for Life's Sake." It is art put to the service of life, but art it is with all its story scored to a contagious musicality that has one reading the story of the lives on the pages while simultaneously singing along in a pitch of sonorous self-story. Such was my experience during the process of writing that essay on *Maud Martha*.

In my case, a poem about my grandmother that had been trying to take form for several years since my grandmother's death, suddenly came to me and went on to win a literary prize. Gwendolyn Brooks inspires readers to move from her great ear for language and her insights to their own struggles for mastery in that regard. Her novel and poetry engage the world in the manner of those great writers who form the African American legacy of *scribes for the people*: Wheatley, Hughes, Petry, Hayden, Morrison, Baldwin, Baraka, Lorde, and on and on and on.

One Christmas eve many years ago when I was a graduate student at Stanford taking a white studies class on the Irish American poet Louise Bogan (who I had come to appreciate for her poem "Men Loved Wholly Beyond Wisdom" and others in *Blue Estuaries*), as I waited in church for Christmas service to begin, saving seats for friends arriving late, I read Bogan's autobiography, *What the Woman Lived*. Thus engrossed, I was suddenly given a jolt when lo and behold, Bogan recounts her experience at a poetry reading in October of 1962, that included a couple of other "canoned" whites and to my delight also the talented Gwendolyn Brooks. Now, about Bogan's fellow "canoned" white poets, Bogan made witticism in the tempo of the vain *New Yorker*, observing "John Berryman read first in a high state of manic excitement. Then me, not bad, and a good response." But in reference to Brooks she had this to say: "Then the dark Miss Gwendolyn Brooks [read her] poems about cockroaches, dead white men, etc."(347). With those words that betrayed Louise Bogan's

"Miss Ann conceit," I lost respect for her as a literary critic. For clearly, Brooks' artful rendering of the life consequences, for those of us who are daily invaded by cockroaches and rats, matches in every way, and *transcends even*, the best of the thumb-sucking, canonized Boganian types whose attachment to "granite" and other lofty concrete anchors is the best they have to offer.

No, this is not a comparison piece on diverse writers of America. What it is, is homage to Gwendolyn Brooks, grateful she once graced the world with her gifted genius. We read her works, we think about life in a way that makes us better able to contend with life, and we look up from her works invigorated by her magic, which like a metronome, readies us for our own songs to take form in verse or prose.

Work Cited

Bogan, Louise. *What the Woman Lived*. Ed. Ruth Limmer. New York: Harcourt Brace Jovanovich, Inc.,1973.

REMEMBERING MS. BROOKS:
A LESSON IN PATIENCE
AND PERSISTENCE

Shirley N. Weber

In the late 1980s, I received a most unusual call from the chair of the Living Writers Series on campus wondering if we would be interested in bringing Gwendolyn Brooks to campus. He had heard that she was going to be in Southern California and might be able to add San Diego to her itinerary. Of course I responded with an enthusiastic "yes."

Immediately we went to work preparing for her visit. We publicized her lecture widely throughout the campus and local community, required our students in the literature classes to become very familiar with her works, planned an elegant book signing reception, and made sure she was properly hosted while in San Diego. We wanted to make this an affair to remember.

As I reflect on the event, I think I was more excited than the students. All my life I had read the works of Gwendolyn Brooks. I had seen her very simple, yet gentle, face on many posters. However, seeing her in person, and feeling her presence was simply wonderful. She was tall and stately with round thick glasses and baby-smooth dark skin that belied her 70 years. There was nothing flashy or showy about her. Some might even say she was rather homey in her appearance. Yet, in her simplicity, she was powerful. Gwendolyn Brooks was just Gwendolyn Brooks.

As I listened to her, I was struck by her strong voice and determined spirit. She read a poem that was a tribute to sisters who still wore natural hairstyles, and immediately we bonded. The revolutionary spirit that fired her poems of the 1940s, and every decade since, was alive and vibrant. I kept wondering, how does one maintain such fire in these times of confusion? How does one remain optimistic during these times of great oppression and deception? Listening and seeing Ms. Brooks, renewed my spirit.

Following her lecture, Ms. Brooks signed books, books, and books. When we tried to end the line, she said, "No." It took hours for her to sign the books because she spoke with each student. And, those students who were aspiring writers were given special attention. Our faculty was amazed at the tremendous amount of time and care Ms. Brooks gave to each person. Everyone left believing this poetic giant had personally touched him or her.

When we finally left the reception, I was exhausted. Ms. Brooks was a bit worn and hungry, too. She wanted some fried chicken. Unfortunately, it was so late that all the places were closed in San Diego. I offered her other cuisines, but she graciously declined. I felt horrible.

When I dropped her off at the hotel, I assured her I would return the next morning before she was scheduled to be taken to the train station. (Ms. Brooks did not travel by air.) As I was driving home, thinking of this grand lady, I had visions of my mother and other such great ladies inspiring me by their strength and their life stories of determination.

Just as I was about to turn onto my block, I decided I

could not let Ms. Brooks get on a train for Chicago without the traditional send off. So, I headed to the grocery store around midnight. I spent the night frying chicken and baking a pound cake. I got out my old picnic basket and prepared the sister an appropriate meal for the long journey: fried chicken, pound cake, assorted juices, breads, crackers, cheese, fruit, etc. She had enough to last all the way to Chicago.

When I went to the hotel the next morning, I insisted that my two small children accompany me. They did not understand why they needed to meet this lady. I told them that in time they would thank me for the experience. Ms. Brooks was surprised to see the basket of home-cooked food. I told her, "I can't let a sister get on a long train ride without her fried chicken." We both laughed. I took pictures of her and my children. We hugged, promised to do this again, and departed. That Christmas, she sent me a lovely card reminiscing about the fried chicken. We exchanged Christmas cards for years to come.

I often think of Ms. Brooks as I struggle with the challenges of chairing the Africana Studies department and making a difference in my writings and work. I think of her when I become impatient with my students who lack focus and perseverance. I remember how she listened to students and discussed their dreams because she did not want to kill their spirit. I think of her often when I feel abandoned and want to give up the work started by the activists of the 1960s and crawl back into my "traditional" discipline where I understand all the rules and don't have to find creative answers to the repetitive question fueled by racism, "What can you do with a degree in Black Studies?" When I feel like giving up, I think of Ms. Brooks—a spirit that never died. I think of her optimism. I see her fiery, yet gentle spirit, her kind demeanor, and I am renewed.

FANFARE FOR THE COMMON POET

REGINA HARRIS BAIOCCHI

I am a Gwendolyn Brooks anecdote: immortalized in a poem I wrote and a composition in which I set a Brooks poem to music. For the last decade of her life whenever I saw Ms. Brooks she reminded me how she fondly and often told the story of reading for my junior high school students. At the time I was teaching math and conducting a choir after school.

One day I suggested my home room students explore African American legends living in Chicago. I shared with my students several letters I had received from Ms. Brooks encouraging me to publish my poetry. Her letters inspired me to respect and explore and develop poetic forms. Through her poems, I discovered that the sonnet, for example—much to the chagrin of popular perception—accommodates African Americana.

In addition to my correspondences with Ms. Brooks, I turned my pupils on to the annual poetry contests Ms. Brooks held with her personal funding. They voted unanimously to invite her to our school for a reading. One thing led to another and we were soon having bake sales, taffy apple and candy drives, and even panhandling to raise her honorarium. I was quite perturbed with the administration because in previous years a check had simply been written to Oscar Peterson for an evening of Jazz and cocktails; but our children were charged with raising money for the first African American Poet Laureate of the state of Illinois, the first African American Pulitzer Prize winner, and celebrant of African American culture. Not that I am against Oscar Peterson; quite the contrary. As a composer and author and Peterson fan, I was disturbed that an affluent private school would treat one aspect of our culture disparagingly, while championing another. I am convinced that the school's administrators' splintered thinking was fueled by gender and genre hierarchies; stature notwithstanding.

It is important in the chronology of this tale to note that Ms. Brooks accepted our invitation immediately on two conditions: (1) I make arrangements through her agent, Mrs. Beryl Zitch; (2) I realize that money was not an object, as she never refused requests from children. While the exact figure of her fee is inconsequential, I stressed a lesson with my students: society pays dearly to hear former US presidents lie, under the guise of lecturing, but school-age children have to wage bake sales to finance the Poet Laureate's stipend.

Ghosts of my childhood echoed, "What if they gave a war and nobody came?" "People buy what they want [fun] and beg for what they need [spiritual bread]." Alms for culture, as we were painfully reminded, seemed the preferred mantra. The flip side is that our culture is always splintered: we must choose one over the other; in this case, jazz over poetry, instead of both. Ironically, the conscious mind knows that jazz can never exist without poetry and vice versa.

Once the news of Ms. Brooks' coming spread, the entire

school lobbied to attend. Being a people of community, we opened up the day to everyone. Plans went from Ms. Brooks' meeting in my home room with 25 students to include 100 junior-high students, then the entire K-8 student body of some 600 students and their parents. By then I was livid that one of our many world-renowned parents of great means didn't offer matching funds to close the bake sale gaps. Each step of the way, Ms. Brooks assured me that whatever we raised would be sufficient. Her gracious assurances did not ease my shame.

On the day of the event, we didn't send a limo to retrieve Ms. Brooks. My husband met her at her modest bungalow at 7428 South Evans in our old rusty jalopy. The journey to and from the school was filled with the warmth of genuine conversation; as if longtime friends were reacquainting.

Having taught as many Brooks' poems as I could in the brief confines of home room classes—and encouraging colleagues to do the same—our school was eager and ready to receive *Our Mrs. Brooks*. Plans called for Ms. Brooks to read and host a Question and Answer period between 1:00 and 2:30 P.M.; dismissal time was 2:45 P.M. As Ms. Brooks read, many primary students, having learned her poetry aurally and orally, recited fervently in unison, despite shushes from teachers and parents. Around 2:00 P.M. a third grader requested Ms. Brooks' autograph. "Sure," she agreed and asked, "Is there anyone else who wants an autograph? I can take care of them now and return to other questions."

The response was phenomenal. Hundreds of white pages were flagged in the air. From 2:00 P.M. to 10:00 P.M., Ms. Brooks sat patiently signing notebooks, scraps of paper and textbooks. Ignited by Ms. Brooks' poetics, a group of parents organized and spread out to local bookstores where they purchased the entire Brooks inventories, including anthologies that contained her poetry. Passersby and pedestrians questioning the object of the swelling crowd crashed our poetry party. Calls were made to other parents who left their jobs from far and yonder and scurried to the assembly with books to be signed.

Even after having the Irish headmaster condescendingly refer to her as "Gwen" (to which she responded by raising his name tag up to the light and sneering "Yes, Tom!") Ms. Brooks inscribed books for eight consecutive hours, refusing coffee breaks, potty breaks or a dinner break; only taking nominal sips of water to ensure hydration. She explained her tenacity simply by saying with a chuckle, "If these (my) children are willing to stand in line for my chicken scratch, the least I can do is sit here and sign."

That day, more than all the countless meetings I had with Ms. Brooks, helped shape my humility as a composer and author. I realize that my words and musical notes remain mere ink blots on a page until performers or readers lend them voice or an ear. It is through this artist-audience courtship—if you will—that life immemorial is breathed into my compositions.

Mrs. Gwendolyn Brooks Blakely's precise hand, though never mistaken for Palmer's Penmanship, is a poem in itself; an anthology of all the things she became: the People's Poet donned in navy blue utilitarian garb; the Children's Poet who described poetry as "life distilled;" the Ever-Teaching Poet whose life and canon embody her poem, "The Artists' and Models' Ball": "Wonders do not confuse. / We call them that / And close the matter there. But common [folks] Surprise us. / They accept the names we give / With calm, and keep them. Easy-breathing then / We brave our next small business. Well, behind / Our backs they alter. How were we to know."

Part Two

THE MOTHER, FRIEND

"I have managed to excite many area youngsters toward a realization that poetry can be nourishing and enhancing and, again, extending. I have not told these youngsters that handling paper and pencil will guarantee a Pulitzer [P]rize. I tell them, chiefly, that poetry, written or read, can enrich and strengthen their lives. I tell that to other sizes of peoples too."

–Gwendolyn Brooks
from *"The Day of the Gwendolyn,"*

REMEMBRANCE OF GWENDOLYN
Margaret T. Burroughs

Dear Henry Jr., Nora, other family members and friends of Gwendolyn Brooks Blakely:

Certainly, you must realize that I share your pain at the passing of your Dear Mother and my Dear Friend, Gwendolyn Brooks Blakely. For more than sixty years, aside from being age mates, Gwendolyn and I have been close friends dating from when we were teenagers. I remember when Gwendolyn, Henry, and I were members of the NAACP Youth Council in the 1930s. We used to meet at the, South Side Women's Y.W.C.A. at 46th and South Parkway, now King Drive.

I remember that it was at one of those meetings that Gwendolyn nudged me to look across the room. "Margaret," she said, "Do you see that young man over there?" "Yes," I answered. I looked across the room and saw a handsome young man who turned out to be Henry Blakely. Gwen continued, "Margaret," she said, pointing at him, "That's the man I'm going to marry!" I then called to the young man, "Hey! Listen up! Henry! This girl is going to marry you!"

Well, I don't know what happened after that, but obviously Henry and Gwen touched bases, the two of them got together, and some time later became Mr. and Mrs.

Remembrances. I will never forget the 1933 march against lynching in which the Youth Council participated. About twenty members carried signs that said, "Stop lynching! Free the Scottsboro boys!" and "Free Willie McGee!" We were to march down South Parkway from 35th Street to 55th Street, led by our sponsor, the beautiful young teacher, Mrs. Francis Taylor Matlock. Robert McGee, now a minister at Bishop Arthur M. Brazier's church [Apostolic Church of God], carried a soapbox. Every other block or so, we would stop and gather around him as he gave the message against lynching. When we got to 51st Street, the police stopped us and demanded to see our permit. We had none. However, Mrs. Matlock was able to charm the policeman, and we were allowed to continue our march.

Remembrances. The close relationship between myself and Gwen continued on and well after our high school years. If I remember correctly, she and I were married in the same year, Gwen to Henry, and me to Bernard Goss. Also, I believe that Gwen and I birthed our firstborns in the same year. Gwen had Henry, Jr. and I had Gayle. Our close friendship continued through Henry, Jr. and Gayle's growing up years, and the birth of Nora.

Remembrances. I remember fondly the meetings of the creative writing class that we had at the South Side Community Art Center in the 1940s. It was taught by Mrs. Inez Cunningham Stark Boulton, who was on the board of *Poetry Magazine*. In this class was Gwendolyn, Henry, myself,

Robert Davis, Margaret Cunningham, and others.

It was Mrs. Boulton who sponsored the poetry contest which first brought Gwendolyn to prominence and public notice. I remember that Gwendolyn won the first prize of $100. Robert Davis won the second prize of $75. Henry won the third prize of $50, and I won the fourth prize of $25.

I remember that both Gwendolyn and Henry were always encouraging to me and [Charles, my second husband] and especially in our efforts to open up the DuSable Museum, (the first black history museum in the United States, in 1961), in our home at 3806 S. Michigan Avenue.

On numerous occasions, I, too, have had the honor of being invited to participate in the many events where Gwendolyn and Henry have been honored. In the 1940s and 1950s, we were members of the South Side Writers Group. We, the members of this Group, were not the least bit surprised when people began to laud Gwendolyn for her extraordinary, literary accomplishments as she began to receive the numerous honors and awards, and especially, the Pulitzer Prize for poetry. You see, we knew way back then that Gwendolyn, with her poetic talent, *was destined for greatness*.

Remembering, yes, the Thanksgiving week when I went along with Gwen and Henry to visit Henry's people somewhere in Illinois, and Henry's car slid into a snow-covered ditch. It was freezing cold, and we feared freezing to death. Luckily, no one was hurt, and the highway patrol pulled us out, and set us on our way.

Remembering, my visits to Gwen and Henry's summer place in Kankakee, and the fierce mosquitoes that I fought around the pond near the cottage.

Remembering visiting Gwen's home at 43rd and

Langley and meeting her gracious Mom and Dad . . . and noting how Gwen's mother, Keziah, encouraged her poetic efforts.

Remembering visiting Gwen and Henry's second floor apartment on East 63rd Street, and later 74th and Champlain, where our writer's group often met and critiqued our poetry and prose.

Remembering one meeting when our anarchist member became enraged at some political event, pulled out a small American flag, and set it afire right there in Henry and Gwendolyn's living room! We were in awe and shock when Gwen hastily doused the fire and invited our anarchist to get out of her house.

Remembering the party that our teacher, Mrs. Boulton, invited us to at her exclusive North side condo, where the elevator operator noted we were black and suggested we take the freight elevator. We phoned Mrs. Boulton, and she came down herself to escort us up. I understand that she had that elevator operator terminated because of his treatment of us.

Remembering the parties that we used to have at the South Side Community Art Center, 3831 South Michigan, and at the Burroughs' coach house studio, 3806 South Michigan, for the purpose of raising funds to support good cultural and social causes. Gwendolyn and Henry always came. It was at such events where we met such cultural luminaries as Langston Hughes, Paul Robeson, Big Bill Broonzy, and many others who took an interest in us young writers and artists.

Remembering a trip I took [to] Dar es Salaam, Tanzania. As I walked passed one of the hotels, who should I run into but my friend, Gwendolyn Brooks! Imagine meeting Gwen away, over there in the motherland! You can imagine how we hugged each other . . .well.

Remembering . . . Gwendolyn's honoring me in 1997 by speaking at my "thirty-ninth" birthday fundraiser at the DuSable Museum! These are a few remembrances.

In conclusion, it has dawned on me that Gwendolyn, and Henry, Sr. too for that matter, will no longer be with me, with us, in the flesh, but both of them will always be with me, with us, in the spirit, for the spirit never dies! Their spirits will live, whenever we repeat Gwendolyn's name, or Henry's, or whenever we read or recite their poetry, they will spring alive. They will live in the same way that Phyllis Wheatley, Langston Hughes, Sterling Brown, Margaret Danner, James Welden Johnson, Frank Marshall Davis, Margaret Walker, and countless others live! Gwendolyn will live through the legacy that she has left, and so will Henry, Sr. By the legacy Gwendolyn and Henry have left to us, they have earned the right to become our honored ancestor spirits.

How fortunate Nora and Henry, Jr. are that Gwendolyn and Henry were their parents and that they were able to be with them for well more than 50 years!

How fortunate all of us are that we have had them as our friends who enriched our lives!

Now, Gwendolyn Brooks Blakely and Henry Blakely, Sr. have ascended into their places as literary stars in the firmament, and we salute them with reverence.

December 11, 2000
Funeral Service
Rockefeller Chapel
University of Chicago

JUST WANTED TO KEEP IN TOUCH
GWENDOLYN A. MITCHELL

Dear Mama Gwendolyn,

I miss you. As I write this note, the year is 2007. It doesn't seem as if you've been gone for seven years, but you have. I don't need to remind you that I work in a place that has made an active commitment to keep your words and works alive, so there are constant reminders of your presence—your books are on the shelves, images of you are on the walls throughout the building, and I have often forwarded requests for your poems to your Brooks permissions office.

When folks come to visit our facility, I always have them stop on the landing in front of your portrait that Murry DePillars painted for your eightieth birthday celebration. Do you remember that day? I was so very fortunate to have been a part of that day's festivities and to have presented you with one of your eighty poetic gifts. I recently went through a stack of old letters and found the note that you sent to me thanking me for my contribution. It should have been me thanking you for your thoughtfulness. You were always so meticulous at sending notes and thank-yous.

I was trying to think of the first time that I met you. I'm quite sure that it was at a Black writers conference that was hosted by Sonia Sanchez and Houston Baker in Philadelphia in the Spring of 1977. I was a senior in college; and Mr. Brown, the director of Penn State's Paul Robeson Cultural Center, took a few students to the conference. That was a life-changing experience for me. It felt like an initiation, and I was welcomed into this marvelous community of Black poets. I then met you again in Dallas a few years later. You gave a reading and conducted a poetry workshop at Southern Methodist University. I was one of the eager poets in the audience who was bold enough to read a poem to which you offered verbal, on the spot critique. As I recall, you were very kind and encouraging. Your words kept me writing.

Over the years, I would make it a point to attend your poetry readings. I loved to hear your voice: the lovely lilts and lows of speech that were and remain distinctly Gwendolyn Brooks. When I finally moved to Chicago in the late 1990s, I thought it was indeed a gift that I would be living in "your" Bronzeville. It's been a privilege to work in the publishing house that publishes your work. In the capacity as editor and employee, I had the delightful task of assisting with some of your local events. And as a fellow poet, I was able, on occasion, to share the stage with you. But I think that the greatest excitement came one day while I was in my office, our publisher and your cultural son, Haki R. Madhubuti, came in full of smiles. He had a note from you and the table of contents for your new poetry book. You had been promising him a new book and now it was closer to becoming a reality. As you know, we were not able to publish your book before you made your transition, but I was delighted to have been able to work with your daughter, Nora, who spent so much time working out the details with you that we felt your spiritual presence during each step of the project. I hope that you like your book. I think it is an elegant compliment to the words that are inside. Thank you for the opportunity to work on *In Montgomery*; I will cherish the time and the experience that it provided.

Mama Gwendolyn, I wish I had had the chance to spend more time with you while you were physically on this earth, but I know through your words and the constant reminders of your presence that you will be with me each time I take pen to page.

I love you.
Your Daughter in the word.

P.S.
I found a copy of the poem that I wrote for your eightieth birthday celebration.

What Mattered Most

Remember, Ms. Brooks?
Once after you read poems
to a crowd in Dallas,
remember how you relinquished the floor
to a room full of younger poets?
You stood, with intensity, thoughtful grace,
hushed the room silent
each time clumsy voices would rise
      to speak
      you led the applause
      offered pieces of advice
      on projection, style, finding voice
      within.
      We took your words,
      like a mother's praise,
      as what mattered most.

          Gwendolyn A. Mitchell

A CHILDLESS MOTHER OR REFLECTIONS ON MOTHERHOOD: GWENDOLYN BROOKS' "THE MOTHER"

GEORGENE BESS MONTGOMERY

I had an abortion. There, I have said it after all of these years. Now, my secret, that only the medical staff and the unborn child knew, is no longer a secret. The unborn child visits me in my dreams and stares back at me accusingly, lovingly through the eyes of my daughter.

When the pregnancy test registered positive behind the locked door of my bathroom, I momentarily cherished the life growing inside of me, the miracle that would transform my body and my life, and connect me to a man I swore to love forever but whose face or name I can now no longer recall. Yet, I never considered not having an abortion. I immediately vowed to develop no feelings for "it." It would become neither a part of my consciousness, my heart, nor my body. That was the healthiest, the safest way I was told. However, that did not free me from an unacknowledged attachment to my child. I repeatedly, without even realizing it, touched my stomach. I wondered whether it was a boy or a girl. Would s/he be a writer, a lover of words and the pen? Part of me longed to tell someone of the life growing inside of me. But I didn't.

More significantly, I didn't want anyone to know that I had had an abortion. What would they think of me, a staunch Pentecostal church member who had judged and condemned others for sinning? What would they think of me, an ordained, praying woman at 12 years old, the youngest praying woman ever? Knowing what goes on in the dark will come to light, I determined to extinguish that light and never let it shine. I certainly never told Gwendolyn Brooks; however, it's as if she were there inside my head and my heart when she wrote her provocative and poignant poem, "the mother," because it so clearly expresses and vividly captures my continuing mental state since and because of that abortion of long ago. Reading Brooks' poem engaged in me an intense self-reflection and remembrances of a long ago abortion, an experience I thought I had forgotten, but as Brooks so succinctly and poignantly reveals, "Abortions will not let you forget" for you will always "remember the children you got that you did not get."

Significantly, Brooks published "the mother" in her collection of poetry, *A Street in Bronzeville*, in 1945, twenty-eight years before the *Roe v. Wade* decision that legalized abortion. Perhaps to help her readers understand and know life on symbolic and metaphoric Bronzeville streets, Brooks recorded what she saw and experienced– the lives lived in quiet desperation, the unending cycle and saga of poverty and hard times, and the difficulty of rearing children who will in turn live the same lives of their parents. In so doing, Brooks presents to us the pains and joys of motherhood, of knowingly bearing children into a world of poverty, where they grow up on the mean streets of life that teach them painful truths about living, loving, and losing. Yet, she also reveals to us the tender side of love such as watching children grow up, fulfill their dreams, and become all they can be. While both the pro-life and pro-choice supporters may read "the mother" as a platform for their positions, Brooks takes not a particular side but provides instead a poignant insight into the realities of motherhood and the abortion decision.

Thus, Brooks' "the mother" explores the notion of motherhood and presents an alternative definition of motherhood. Although the speaker does not specifically raise the following questions (1) Does motherhood occur at the moment of conception? (2) Is motherhood giving birth?(3) If a woman has an abortion, does that her a mother make? (4) Does abortion negate motherhood? The poem's details answer them.

For Brooks, it seems, a woman is a mother simply because she conceives. Abortion revokes not a woman's motherhood card, for the "dim killed children," who have never had the light shine on them, who have never been in the light but existed only in the dark womb, in the grayness of unclear thinking and (in)decision, who were aborted, are always with her. Because she addresses her readers through her effective and deliberate use of "you," the speaker universalizes the experience of abortion; no one, not even men, is exempt.

That Brooks entitled her poem "the mother," the more formal term for the female parent, but wrote it in lower-case letters, suggests Brooks' subtle commentary on and distinction between mother and the more familiar "mama." Mother is one who bears a child; mama is one who feeds, nurtures, disciplines, kisses, cares for, tends to, fusses over, sits up late waiting for, worries about, and spends her last dime on her children.

Without judgment or condemnation and with an insider's insight, "the mother" is a soliloquy to the unborn child. Alternately, the childless mother/speaker apologizes, explains, remembers, imagines, relives, offers embraces, and wishes as she recalls the unborn children, the "damp small pulps with a little or with no hair / The singers and workers that never handled the air." Like Sethe in Toni Morrison's *Beloved*, the childless mother accepts responsibility and acknowledges her (mis)deeds. Addressing her not born child, she offers subtle apology and explanation for the taking of life, for the denial of life's loves, losses, joys, pains, uncertainties and expectations:

> ...Sweets, if I sinned, if I seized
> Your luck
> And your lives from your unfinished reach,
> If I stole your births and your names,
> . . . .
> Your stilted or lovely loves, your tumults, your
> marriages aches and your deaths,
> If I poisoned the beginnings of your breaths,
> Believe that even in my deliberateness I was not
> deliberate. (17-25)

Yet even as the speaker explains, she chastises herself for whining, for what is done is done, and done by her: "Though why should I whine, / Whine that the crime was other than mine?— / Since anyhow you are dead. / Or rather, or instead, / You were never made." Continuing her internal debate, she notes, "But that too, I am afraid, / Is faulty: oh, what shall I say, how is the truth to be said?/ You were born, you had body, you died. / It is just that you never giggled or planned or cried."

The reader wonders if the speaker is now a mother and has thus experienced the deepness, the intensity of a mother's love, or does she know intuitively how deeply a mother loves her child(ren)? She describes so vividly a mother's delicious love for her children and regrets as she recognizes that as a consequence of our decision and subsequent action, we "will never . . . scuttle off ghosts that come" in the night scaring our children from their slumber, and that we "will never leave them, controlling [our] luscious sigh, / Return for a snack of them, with gobbling mother-eye." She hears her conscience in the "voices of the wind the voices of my dim killed/children." While she did not give birth, her body has "contracted" as if giving birth. In her mind and her heart, she has "eased / My dim dears at the breasts they could never suck."

Ending her one-sided conversation with the gotten but ungotten children, the speaker expresses her love for those children. Just because she didn't give birth doesn't mean she didn't love them, want them, remember them, or treasure them. Perhaps not sure they will accept her apology, explanation, or proclamation of love, she beseeches "Believe me, I loved you all. / Believe me, I knew you, though faintly, and I loved, I loved you /All."

Is it possible to love children whom you choose to deny life, to abort their living and loving? Is it possible to not forget the short-lived lives that never really were? Is it possible to hear in the wind the voices of those who couldn't survive our decision? Is it possible to see in the eyes of others, the shadows, the ghosts of children past? Is it possible? For the childless mother in Brooks' "the mother," and for those of us who made the sacrifice, the answer is yes. We never forget. We always remember. We always love. We always feel, hear, taste, long for, see, and smell those who are not here. I certainly do.

Now, I am a mother. I have an incredibly beautiful ten-year old daughter, Zora Indigo, who loves to sing, dance, wear wigs, laugh, talk to her dolls, do hair, put on make-up, walk around the house in my shoes and clothes, and write poems and short stories. Her plans for her future—her chosen profession, the college of her choice, what kind of clothes, shoes, and wigs she will wear, how many children she'll have, and where she'll live—change daily. But what is constant is her love for me and my love for her. Each time I hold her, kiss her, tell her "I love you," discipline her, praise her, I do so in the shadowed memory of the child I chose not to have. And I love my Zora Indigo all the much more, for she is my second chance, my second chance to do the right thing, to make the right decision, to choose life. No longer just a mother, I am now a "mama."

Work Cited

Brooks, Gwendolyn. *A Street in Bronzeville*. New York: Harper & Brothers, 1945.

PART THREE
THE TEACHER

MAUD MARTHA

...issed, quarreled,
...folk who were
...ould be.

...magazines

...cts there

..., th...ing

...ays of

...res of ro... with wood

...oftly glowing, touched... y the compliment of a spot of auburn here, the low burn of a
rare binding there. There were ferns in these
rooms, and Chinese boxes; bits of dreamlike crys-
tal; a taste of leather. In the adverti... ages,
you saw where you could buy six It...
eleven hundred dollars—and you
there was just the one set; you saw
buy antique Fre... ch bisque figuri...
gold... fo... or... H... whole b...
...l... on... thes...
...r... eciall...
...wea...

"Certain writers are characterized by particular powers and graces. Even though their subjects may be similar to the subjects of others, <u>if they are daring</u>—(and a writer who wants to be truthful, who wants to Reach, has got to be daring)—their animating hands upon clay are absolutely like <u>no other</u> hands upon clay."

–Gwendolyn Brooks
from "Introductions to Speakers at the Library of Congress, 1985-1986"

GWENDOLYN BROOKS –
AN APPRECIATION
PAULE MARSHALL

In the early 1950s, as a fledgling fiction writer, I learned invaluable lessons from Gwendolyn Brooks' slender and poetic novel, *Maud Martha*, that had just been published at the time. In terms of craft and technique, *Maud Martha* taught me restraint and economy in the use of language, as well as the importance of specificity–that is, the authenticating details that are the lifeblood of fiction. In addition, there was her skillful characterization. Her young heroine, Maud Martha, appears to be just another struggling Chicago mother and housewife. Yet, in Brooks' hands, she possesses a rich and complex inner life that makes her an extraordinary creation. For me, Maud Martha was one of the first black women in fiction to be given her full weight and substance as a character. She was a powerful and necessary answer to the limited, largely stereotype image portrayed in white, mainstream literature. Brooks' in-depth portrayal of both "the body and soul" of her heroine provided me with a model that would guide me as a novelist over the years. Gwen, poet and novelist, pointed the way and, for that, I remain in her debt.

GWENDOLYN BROOKS AS THE BRIDGE OVER THE GENERATIONS

MOLEFI KETE ASANTE

I remember when I first met Gwendolyn Brooks. I was a young professor at UCLA. As the Director of the Center for African American Studies, I had chauffeured her around the city from one appointment to another. She was gracious, kind, thoughtful, and wise. I thought of her as the sum total of all of our wisdom as a people, the apex of what it means to be a writer, the beauty of our nobility against racism, and the bridge between the generations. I said to her, eager to get an answer from someone so famous, so smart, and so committed to African people, "What do you think about the Harlem Renaissance?" Oh, how now I see how dumb the question was, how innocent I was, and yet how generous she was to answer me. She said, "the Harlem Renaissance was a group of black writers reading their works to white people. The real revolution in writing is going on right now in the streets and in the community centers in the black communities where young poets, like Don Lee (Haki Madhubuti) are reading to our people." This was 1972. I never forgot it, and I have always wanted to connect with my people the same way, knowing that the only way we could ever have an African resurgence is when we advance with our people. Writers must first of all write for their own people, that is the truth of universality. I am indebted to Gwendolyn Brooks for being a bridge for me.

I met her next in 1987 in Philadelphia. James Baldwin was also in town, and since I had written the playbill for Baldwin's *Amen Corner* to be performed at the Annenberg Theater at the University of Pennsylvania, I was invited to dinner with Baldwin, Gwendolyn Brooks, Houston Baker, and two students at the home of Rowena Stewart, head of the African American Museum in Philadelphia. The evening started pleasant enough, but after an hour or so, James Baldwin was quite drunk, probably drinking to drown out his pain, mental and physical. Gwendolyn Brooks sat sage-like observing Baldwin's antics. He berated the American government for its racism, imperialism, and sexism. He condemned the people who give literary prizes and said that no person who tells the truth to racists will ever be awarded any real recognition. He praised the French, spoke of the *Croix de Guerre* which he had received from the French and said that nothing like that had ever happened for him in America. I recall Gwendolyn, Houston, and myself trying to console him, to talk sense into him, basically saying that it did not matter that the whites had not rewarded him because we had rewarded him in our own hearts. I told him that he had to live to be respected and honored among his own people; they would make his name live forever. Gwendolyn Brooks broke through to him, I believe, when she said to him that the best thing he could do was to "forget the French and the Americans and concentrate on your writings, write what you believe and what you feel. In fact, I thought that was what you always did anyway."

Baldwin sort of got some sense from what Gwendolyn was saying. I knew that this great woman, with the precision of her speech and the focus of her mind, could zero in on anything that she wanted and say it in such powerfully plain words that you had to listen. That night, in Washington Square, Philadelphia, I learned something about the greatness of Gwendolyn Brooks, her emotional attachment to the idea of saving black people. She reached deep to try to save James Baldwin, but in doing so, perhaps she saved me and the others, too.

GWENDOLYN BROOKS:
LEAVING HER MARK ON US

JOANNE V. GABBIN

The last time I hosted Gwendolyn Brooks in Virginia was in October 1999. At the invitation of the University of Virginia Press and James Madison University, she had traveled from Chicago by train to Charlottesville to help launch my book, *The Furious Flowering of African American Poetry*. After spending time with Gwendolyn at a lovely dinner party at the home of the director of the Press, the next morning I went to pick her up at the Omni Hotel in downtown Charlottesville. We were to travel over the mountain to Harrisonburg, sixty miles away, where she was scheduled to do a 10 o'clock reading at James Madison University. She was slow to come downstairs. I anxiously looked at my watch and was relieved to see that it was only 8:15 A.M. When Gwendolyn finally appeared, she was neatly dressed in a gray suit with a blue and gray plaid blouse. She wore a navy blue knit cap that encircled a leaner, yet still lively face. Her eyebrows arched to her question, "Do I look presentable?" "You look wonderful," I said, as I guided her to my little Nissan and apologized that she would have to stoop low to get into it.

On the way over Afton Mountain, I was relaxed; we were making good time. The fall foliage was at its peak of color. The morning fog, so common to the area, had already burned off to reveal an intensely blue sky. The conversation came easily. She told me about her morning ritual that involved taking the juice of a lemon and a lime with a little honey. She said that it cleansed the system. She offered that it may help me with my own health regimen. We talked about Chicago, George Kent, the Chicago State University center in her name, Nora, and her performance company called Chocolate Chips. I was so enjoying the conversation that I did not heed the flashing traffic sign that warned of a backup due to an accident near Exit 235 on Interstate 81. Before I could get off the highway we were in a 10-mile-backup caused by an overturned tractor-trailer.

My composure gone, my mind racing to come up with a solution to get us to the campus on time, I fell silent. After inching along in traffic for more than forty-five minutes, we managed to get to a rest stop so that I could make a call and let the waiting audience know that we would be delayed. I parked the car and hurried to the phone, leaving the door open. I was gone for several minutes as I made contingency plans. We would not make the 10 o'clock reading. When I returned to the car, Gwendolyn Brooks said, in a way that startled and saddened me, "Joanne, don't ever leave me again like that." For the first time during the entire visit, I was aware of an 82-year-old woman who felt very vulnerable. And I promised not to leave her.

When we finally arrived at JMU, the audience was waiting, and she gave a wonderful reading. We honored her with the dedication of the Furious Flower Center. She took several of us to lunch at a local restaurant that specializes in desserts. She insisted we try at least two. We then got in the car and traveled back to Charlottesville for a reading at the University of Virginia that night. When Gwendolyn Brooks finally mounted the stage to the thunderous applause of eight hundred people crowded in Old Cabell Hall, I watched her steps, slower and more tentative than I remembered, and thought about strength and vulnerability, about infirmity and firmness of spirit, about aging and ageless grace. She ended her reading with a poem that had become one of her favorite finale-poems, "Infirm":

> Everybody here
> is infirm.
> Everybody here is infirm.
> Oh. Mend me. Mend me. Lord.
>
> Today I
> say to them
> say to them
> say to them, Lord:
> look! I am beautiful, beautiful with
> my wing that is wounded
> my eye that is bonded
> or my ear not funded
> or my walk all a-wobble.
> I'm enough to be beautiful.
>
> You are
> beautiful too.

Gwendolyn Brooks had filled us with the certainty that we were all beautiful. The magic of the evening continued until after midnight. She signed books and made a personal connection with every person waiting in a line that ran the length of the hall. Her magnanimous spirit of generosity and encouragement left a mark on all of us. She taught us that we are all vulnerable and strong, and if we are fortunate we can capture all of that in a poem.

NO WASTE:
GWENDOLYN BROOKS'S
LAST WORKSHOP

Quraysh Ali Lansana

I moved to Chicago in 1988, leaving behind an ugly experience in broadcast journalism and the contempt for the state of Oklahoma only natives can truly appreciate. I arrived with two suitcases, a folder full of poems, and big dreams of reinventing myself as a poet in the city that fed some of my guiding lights: Malcolm X, Haki Madhubuti, and Gwendolyn Brooks.

In 1994, while working with the programming committee of Guild Complex, one of the Midwest's most significant literary centers, I was asked to help develop an idea Ms. Brooks was cooking up with Complex founder, poet Michael Warr. She wanted to hold an annual open mic poetry contest and award the winner of said contest $500 of her own monies. Not Illinois Poet Laureate cache, but a personal check from her pocketbook. This is how I met Ms. Brooks, swaddled in the democracy and generosity of her spirit.

Two years later, while driving her home after the third Gwendolyn Brooks Open Mic Award contest, I mentioned I was considering a return to academia to complete my B.A., abandoned in 1985 at the University of Oklahoma. She enthusiastically reminded me that Professor Haki Madhubuti, her publisher and founder of Third World Press, was at Chicago State University and that I should look no other place. I was reserved about her suggestion initially, remembering my bankrupt attempt of a manuscript Third World Press rejected only a year earlier. Noting my hesitation, Ms. Brooks offered to speak with him about school, not my manuscript.

Neither Ms. Brooks nor I knew at the time that within a year we would workshop weekly in the conference room of the center created in her honor.

Madhubuti founded the Gwendolyn Brooks Center for Black Literature and Creative Writing at Chicago State University in 1990. He also initiated the Brooks Conference for Writers of African Descent in the same year. I had met Professor Madhubuti previously, on the floor of his flagship bookstore and African-centered school. He was, and remains, what many of my Black male friends want to be when we grow up: a builder of positive reality.

In Spring 1997, Ms. Brooks sat with eleven young poets of varying levels every Tuesday evening for two hours. It was joy. It was torture. It was Professor Madhubuti who convinced Ms. Brooks to lead this semester-long poetry workshop. Unfortunately it was to be her last.

Ms. Brooks in workshop was a marvel and a wonder. She was an igniter of mind riots. She dropped morsels of ideas: clippings from newspapers, poems by authors she admired, assignments in traditional forms, then sat back and watched us scramble, scrap, and heave. All the while a mischievous, wide grin on her dimpled face, rubbing her hands in delight. She loved instigating, agitating. My work benefited from her firm nudging. It also benefited from her fierce red pen.

Ms. Brooks made it very clear, revision is a part of the creative process, and clearly her work is proof of that mantra. She did not believe in waste. Hers was a hand of precision, and she often spoke of laboring for months over a single word.

The piece that begins with the short poem by Langston Hughes (eventually entitled "baggage") was inspired by the work of my close friend, Christopher Stewart. What is printed here is a later draft, very close to the way the poem appears in my first book. In one of the many earlier drafts, Ms. Brooks commented on the fifth stanza by writing:

> "not 'slipping' into? Doesn't an 'orifice' have a wall?
> Wouldn't that prevent <u>through</u>—slipping?"

How hard-headed was I? The edits she suggests here fail to manifest in the final version. On the same draft she wrote the following regarding the sixth stanza:

> "rich, fatty soul food is also soft, so
> teeth could hardly be cut upon it."

These lines remain unchanged in the draft printed here. However, I finally caught on for the published version:

> or would you collect them,
> while struggling to remember
> the stuff that makes us whole.

smolder

Aunt 'Ree has lived
through the mississippi red
of white sheeted men
staining family hands

she say
he got a white face
but he got blood
just like mine

while a cross burns
the meeting place of her salvation,
she prays for better days
in the ashes of 1996

Quraysh Ali Lansana

baggage

When you turn the corner
And you run into yourself
Then you know that you have turned
All the corners that are left

"Final Curve" by Langston Hughes

what if you woke up one day
and all of your blunders had left you?
your poor judgment calls
your lack of good sense
a lifetime of mistakes
parading around the living room
as you stare in subconscious awe

the money you stole from between your parent's mattresses
while looking for the true detective magazines

the distress call you sent out on the cb radio
that hailed ten unhappy truck drivers to your front door

the lie you told your lover
to conceal your other lover

would you feel them departing?
slipping through any available orifice
leaving you lightheaded and stain-free?

or would you collect them
while struggling to remember
cutting your teeth on this pain
this rich, fatty soul food

the stuff that makes us whole

Quraysh Ali Lansana

Revised 5/1/97

Additionally, Ms. Brooks and I tinkered with the second stanza of the draft printed here, and ultimately agreed to jettison "the mattresses of mom and dad" for "your parents' mattresses."

Addressing current events in verse was important to Ms. Brooks, as any student of her work is acutely aware. "smolder" was born not only of an assignment, but of the evening news hitting literally very close to home.

1995 and 1996 saw a rash of Black church bombings, in mostly Southern states, but a few in the North and Midwest as well. The First Baptist Church of Enid, Oklahoma, located three blocks west of the church in which I was raised, was leveled by a slightly disturbed gentleman who claimed he was simply "copy-catting." Regardless of his motives, he displaced and disrupted the lives of many relatives and old family friends. My people were on edge for weeks. I penned the first drafts (the first stanza and most of the final stanza in the version printed here) in Chicago.

Perhaps a month after the First Baptist bombing I went home for a visit. While sitting in the cluttered, historic landmark that was the living room of my eccentric aunt, the late Marie Adams (we called her Aunt Ree'), I realized the depth of her struggle to forgive (one of the cornerstones of Christianity) this crazy dude who blew up any church, let alone a church in our hometown:

> he got a white face
> but he got blood
> just like mine

Ms. Brooks immediately gravitated toward the quote. It

made the poem human, personal. Something that was second nature for her. Her comments on the bottom of the page refer to edits I implemented for the third stanza. In an earlier draft, the poem closes:

> while a cross burns
> the saints meeting place
> she prays for better days
> in the ashes of 1996

The draft printed here seems unwieldy, particularly the second line. She compared the drafts, and, after much discussion, we met in the middle for the finished product:

> aunt ree has lived
> through the mississippi
> of sheeted heads
> soiling family hands
>
> she say
> he got a white face
> but he got blood
> just like mine
>
> she prays for better days
> in the ashes of 1996
> while a cross burns
> the saints' meeting place

At the conclusion of the semester, the class, now the Gwendolyn Brooks Writers Collective and only nine in number, initiated a tradition by taking Ms. Brooks out to dinner. She reciprocated, inviting us to a meal that next Christmas. It was at our Spring/Summer outing in 1999 that her ill-health was becoming apparent. She was very frail, and, uncharacteristically for Ms. Brooks, did not have much of an appetite. We worried that she didn't like the restaurant. Professor Madhubuti, who was always very protective of Ms. Brooks, was more tight-lipped than usual.

In August, my wife Emily, my two sons (now four) and I went to visit Ms. Brooks at her condo the day before we moved to New York City. I had been accepted to the MFA Creative Writing Program at NYU, a graduate school journey Ms. Brooks helped initiate and further. She was weak and clearly in pain, though gracious and playful as always. She loved my sons, and demanded to be either the first or second person phoned upon their births. She was second for both. The photo I shot of her with Emily, Nile and Onam sitting on her piano bench is bittersweet joy. It is one of the last photos of Ms. Brooks. She joined the ancestors three and a half months later.

I've led workshops, taught classes or held meetings in her conference room, the conference room of the Gwendolyn Brooks Center, almost every day for the past several academic years. It is both an honor and a chore. But, most of all, I love to open the door to the Center when no one is in but the two of us.

SO THE WORLD MIGHT CONTINUE: IN PRAISE OF GWENDOLYN BROOKS

MAGGIE ANDERSON

The world might continue. Go on with your preparations:
moving among the quick and the dead;
nourishing here, there,
pressing a hand
among the ruins
and among the
seeds of restoration.

–Gwendolyn Brooks,"Collage for Today"

What I most admire in the poems of Gwendolyn Brooks are her sharp-eyed observations of human behavior. From her very first book, *A Street in Bronzeville*, the vital center of Gwendolyn Brooks' poetry is a neighborhood, a community of people passing their daily lives through love and danger, through strict routine and small surprise, in the warmth of human closeness. It is no accident that so many of Brooks' books and single poems feature a person, a character, through whose perspicacity we see the world: Annie Allen, Maud Martha, Emmett Till's mother, or little Lincoln West. Her collected works constitute a chorus of many voices she drew forth from history, from the newspapers, from the stories others told her, and from her own life. "My religion is PEOPLE. LIVING...," Brooks wrote in the second volume of her autobiography, *Report from Part Two* (148). Those living people are everywhere in her work.

As a young poet, I found in Gwendolyn Brooks' poems the wallow, the drag, the uplift of human life, and I found it empowering. I discovered in her poems a permission to speak about or in the voices of the people I knew from my growing up in West Virginia. From the pages of her books, she taught me that it was acceptable to write of the so-called "little people," the invisible people, the vital human lives in the margins. As I read of her "Pool Players Seven at the Golden Shovel," her "Kitchenette People," "the little booths at Benvenuti's," and the more than 2,000 souls who lived "In the Mecca," I began to recognize my own people and my own places as sources for poems. I started to write of the tiny railroad towns of West Virginia, of my contrary grandmother, of the miners and mill workers who were my uncles, and of my aunts who worked too hard all week and sang in church on Sunday. The poems of Gwendolyn Brooks made my own poems possible.

Much later, I met Gwendolyn Brooks-the-person, and I discovered how sincerely interested she was in the people she met in her travels. I think she found us human beings to be bold, puzzling, strong, funny, and passing strange—"unusual," she might have said. When Gwendolyn Brooks turned her wry eye and her questioning, inimitable voice on someone to say, "Oh, you think that, do you?" we were in the presence of a rare, curious intelligence. To be listened to by Gwendolyn Brooks was most of all, as she might have written in capital letters, to be CONSIDERED. I love her precisely qualified formulation of the sources of poetry:

> So much is involved in the writing of poetry—and sometimes, although I don't like suggesting it is a magic process, it seems you really do have to go into a *bit* of a trance...because "brainwork" seems unable to do it all....The self-cast trance is possible when you are *importantly* excited about an idea, or surmise, or emotion.
>
> (*Report from Part One*, 183)

The Gwendolyn Brooks I knew as a person was always "importantly excited" by human interaction, by what folks do. When I consider the influence her work and life have had on me as a writer, I cannot overlook a very particular act of consideration and attention she paid to me in the summer of 1976 at a writers' conference in West Virginia. There was an open poetry reading in the afternoon and Brooks was sort of "officiating." It had been going on for about an hour and the poems had a sameness of both theme and form that had become a bit numbing. I was far too timid to volunteer to read, though the friends I was sitting with kept trying to cajole me into it. Brooks eventually turned to us and asked, "Do any of you have something to read?" My friends, who were not writers themselves, pushed me toward the stage. Later, Brooks looked for me again to ask if I had completed a book of poetry. I lied (as I believe I was expected to) that I did, and she offered to read it. I went home and tried to turn all the poems I had written into something that looked like a book worthy of the consideration of Gwendolyn Brooks. Within a few weeks, she wrote me a letter, saying that she liked the book very much and had sent it to her editor at Harper and Row with a cover letter of recommendation.

Nearly eighteen months later, Harper and Row accepted *Years That Answer*, my first book of poems. During that long wait, Gwen wrote to me regularly to tell me not to be discouraged, to suggest that "no news is good news," and to sign off with her ever-positive, "Hold On!" or "Keep On!" When the book was published in 1980, I invited Gwen to Moundsville, West Virginia, where I was working as a poet-in-residence. We celebrated with a good lunch and a reading she gave at the West Virginia Maximum Security Prison for Men the old "State Pen" where she and I were the only women in the room. I remained in touch with her until just several months before her passing in December of 2000. I considered her a friend, and I believe she enjoyed the letters I wrote her over the years, in which I always tried to find some interesting human detail that might amuse or surprise her. She extended a hand of friendship and support to me at a crucial moment in my life. Like so many others who have experienced her generosity, I know my life as a writer and as a human being was in many ways defined by her spontaneous gesture of affirmation.

Each time I am presented with the opportunity to offer some assistance (asked or unasked) to a younger writer, I think of Gwendolyn Brooks. I think of her as I work with the Wick Poetry Center at Kent State University, which exists, primarily, to offer poetry scholarships, readings, publishing opportunities, and workshops to young and emerging writers.

I still cannot imagine how Gwen ever managed to keep up with her voluminous correspondence, but I know that she did. She not only answered my letters, but she sent me each of her books as gifts. The last package I received from her came in summer 1996. It included a signed copy of *Report from Part Two*, a program from her husband's funeral service, and this brief note: "At last! My book! I hope you'll find in it this-and-that of interest. As you can see from the enclosure, I've been busy. HOLD ON" (private correspondence, July 28, 1996). Her loyal consideration and attention to others–especially to the young and, as she once said in an interview, to "the hidden struggler" (*Report from Part One*, 144)–remain an inspiration to me. "My religion is kindness," Gwendolyn Brooks has written. As a recipient of her extraordinary kindness to a stranger, I thank her forever for the lift she gave to me and for the legacy of her own wonderful poems of her people.

GWENDOLYN ELIZABETH BROOKS
ADELE S. NEWSON-HORST

About seventeen years ago, shortly after earning the Ph.D. in American Literature, I landed a tenure-track position at a predominately white, eastern, liberal arts institution. With an enrollment of nearly 5,000 students from mostly well-to-do backgrounds, the school was a model for both liberal arts education and civic engagement. It was the kind of institution the wealthy with social consciousness might elect to send their children.

The town itself was insular, predominately white, and working class. The University availed to the community a great many cultural events including concerts, guest lectures, and poetry readings. It was at one such event that I first experienced Gwendolyn Brooks.

Sitting in the middle row of lecture-like seating in a huge auditorium, I noted the sheer number of people filing in as well as the diversity of disciplines represented. From Art to Physics, Chemistry to English, the faculty was in attendance in a huge way that evening. There were also the usual "artsy" students in attendance, the less descript ones, and the Greeks. I surmised that they were going to enjoy extra credit points for attending the reading. The community was out in force as well. Some members of the community sat together while others interspersed among faculty and students; however, they clearly stood out as townies.

When the room filled, the lights were dimmed. I knew what Gwendolyn Brooks looked like from the photos on the jacket covers of her volumes, but that did not prepare me for what I saw that night. I knew her poetry as well. Even at this time, Brooks ranked among the authors found in anthologies of American literature, and she was almost always taught in my undergraduate and graduate courses—with the distinction of being the first African American poet to win the Pulitzer Prize for her 1949 volume *Annie Allen*. My mentor is fond of saying that when the academy teaches Black topics, it teaches "the first" as though firsts represent history, art, and thought. Nevertheless, I knew Gwendolyn Brooks as the artist who loved "working with language, as others liked working with paints and clay, or notes." That is, I had an intellectual concept of her as a profoundly rich and exacting poet, but I didn't have a "lived" experience of her.

Entering from the left, Gwendolyn Brooks appeared to be as small as a middle school child. Questioning (or anticipatory) silence immediately swept the room. She walked with her head erect; soft, short curls framing her face called attention to the black glasses. Apparently, she did not need or did not want, an introduction. What appeared to be a concentrated spotlight beamed on her lone figure. Upon reaching the podium, she effortlessly lowered the microphone. Next, she slowly swept the room with clear and keen eyes before speaking. I imagined that she saw me and everyone in the audience, but that could not have been possible given the lighting.

I remember thinking about an interview during which Gwendolyn Brooks said she wanted to write poetry that was "non-compromising"—poems that would be meaningful to Black people. With books titled *A Street in Bronzeville*, *Maud Martha*, *The Bean Eaters*, *In the Mecca*, etc., what, I thought, does this 70-year-old Black woman have to say to this curious assemblage of humanity? I then decided she had orchestrated the silence of the audience to prepare them to receive her message.

"We real cool…," Gwendolyn Brooks announced in clear, crisp, well-modulated timbres. But it wasn't simply the sound of her voice that enchanted, it was the strength of the voice emanating from her small frame. It was the message, the messenger, and the courage to deliver flawlessly that spoke to me.

Gwendolyn Brooks had something Black to say, like Zora Neale Hurston before her, without rancor or apology. In reading the various poems spanning many decades, she celebrated culture, human foibles, tragedy, and love while she invited listeners to join the feast. And they did. For nearly two hours, the audience sat engaged—laughing when appropriate, sighing when appropriate, and engaging Brooks' lived experiences.

I believe I became a better teacher for the experience. Good teaching is, after all, a matter of sharing the life and passion of thought and inviting the student to share in, revise, and own the experience.

Now, when I think of Gwendolyn Brooks, I think of the power to live experience through language.

The Egg Boiler

Being you, you cut your poetry from wood.
The boiling of an egg is heavy art.
You come upon it as an artist should,
With rich-eyed passion, and with straining heart.
We fools, we cut our poems out of air,
Night color, wind soprano, and such stuff.
And sometimes weightlessness is much to bear.
You mock it, though, you name it Not Enough.
The egg, spooned gently to the avid pan,
And left the strict three minutes, or the four,
Is your Enough and art for any man.
We fools give courteous ear—then cut some more,
Shaping a gorgeous Nothingness from cloud.
You watch us, eat your egg, and laugh aloud.

Gwendolyn Brooks
from *The Bean Eaters*

CONTRIBUTORS

CONTRIBUTORS

MAGGIE ANDERSON is the author of four books of poems, most recently *Windfall: New and Selected Poems* (2000). Anderson is also the editor of the new and selected poems of Louise McNeill and co-editor of *Learning by Heart: Contemporary American Poetry about School and A Gathering of Poets*, an anthology of poems read on the twentieth anniversary of the shootings of students at Kent State and Jackson State University in 1973. Currently Maggie Anderson is professor of English at Kent State University, where she directs the Wick Poetry Center and edits the Wick Poetry Series of the Kent State University Press.

MOLEFI KETE ASANTE is professor, Department of African American Studies, at Temple University. Considered by his peers to be one of the most distinguished contemporary scholars, Dr. Asante has published more than sixty books. Recent titles include *The History of Africa: The Quest for Eternal Harmony* (2007), *Cheikh Anta Diop: An Intellectual Portrait* (2007), *Race, Rhetoric, and Identity: The Architecton of Soul* (2005), *Erasing Racism: The Survival of the American Nation* (2003), *Ancient Egyptian Philosophers* (2003), *Scattered to the Wind, Custom and Culture of Ancient Egypt* (2003), and *100 Greatest African Americans* (2002). He is Editor of *Encyclopedia of Black Studies* (with Ama Mazama), Series Editor of *Routledge Studies on Africa* and Series Editor (with Toyin Falola and Berkeley Eddins) of Humanities Books *Classic Texts in African American History*. Dr. Asante is the founding Editor of

Journal of Black Studies. His work on African culture and philosophy has been cited by *Imhotep*, *Journal of Communication*, *Western Journal of Black Studies*, *Afrocentric Scholar*, and *Journal of Black Studies.* He has published more than 300 journal and magazine articles. The founder of the theory of Afrocentricity, Dr. Asante's books, *Afrocentricity*; *The Afrocentric Idea*; and *Kemet, Afrocentricity and Knowledge* are key works in the field.

REGINA HARRIS BAIOCCHI is an author and a composer. Her music has been performed internationally by various ensembles including: Detroit Symphony Orchestra, Chicago Symphony Orchestra, and the United States Army Band.

Ms. Baiocchi's byline appears in Oxford University Press's second edition of the encyclopedia *Black Women in America*, *AIM Magazine*, *ESI*, and *Technology News*. Her poem, "Teeter totter," received honorable mention in a state-wide competition sponsored by *Chicago Tribune Magazine*. She is featured in the *New Grove Dictionary of American Music*, on the cover of *From Symphonies to Spirituals*, and at HistoryMakers.com.

Ms. Baiocchi teaches in the Liberal Education Department at Columbia College Chicago. Her fiction and poetry have been praised by Gwendolyn Brooks, Nikki Giovanni, Lee Bey, Studs Terkel, Haki Madhubuti, Angela Jackson, Calvin Forbes, Kalamu ya Salaam, and Toni Morrison. Regina Harris Baiocchi is the author of *Indigo Sound* and *Urban Haiku & Other Selected Poems*.

MARGARET TAYLOR GOSS BURROUGHS is completely dedicated to the creative arts, international culture, and specifically to African and African-American life, history and tradition. She is the author of the books, *Jasper the Drummin' Boy* (1947), *Did you feed my Cow?* (1955), and several more in recent years. Her numerous articles concerning art, culture, and history appear in *Chicago Schools Journal*, *Elementary English Journal*, *School Arts Magazine*, *Freedomways*, *Black World*, *The Associated Negro Press* and other numerous publications.

Dr. Burroughs is a strong and devout believer in cultural and historical organizations and is founder of the South Side Community Art Center. She is the originator of the Lake Meadows Outdoor Art Fair and she serves as its Annual Director. In 1959, Dr. Burroughs organized the National Conference of Artists at Atlanta (Georgia) University and served as Chairperson of that organization.

For several years, she was Art Director and Assistant in Research for the Negro History Hall of Fame, sponsored by the *New Crusader* Newspaper in Chicago. In 1961, she helped organize the Museum of Negro History and Art, now known as the DuSable Museum of African American History, and served until 1985 as its Executive Director. She was appointed as a Commissioner to the Chicago Park District Board by the late Mayor Harold Washington in 1985, and reappointed by Acting Mayor Eugene Sawyer in 1987 to a five-year term that ended in 1993. However, Mayor Richard M. Daley reappointed her for another term that ended in 1998, and again for a term that ended in 2003. Mayor Daley reappointed her again for yet another term which will end in 2008. Today, she serves as Chairperson of the Committee on Programs and Recreation as well as a member of the Committee on Capital Improvements.

Dr. Burroughs was married for over forty years to Charles Burroughs (deceased February, 1994), was Co-Founder of the DuSable Museum (she currently serves as Director Emeritus), has two children (Gayle, deceased July 2002), six grandchildren, and loves cats.

JOANNE V. GABBIN is the Executive Director of the Furious Flower Poetry Center and professor of English at James Madison University. She is author of *Sterling A. Brown: Building the Black Aesthetic Tradition*, which was published in a new edition by the University Press of Virginia in 1994, *The Furious Flowering of African American Poetry* (1999), *Furious Flower: African American Poetry from the Black Arts Movement to the Present* (2004), and a children's book, *I Bet She Called Me Sugarplum* (2004).

Dr. Gabbin has published essays in *Wild Women in the Whirlwind*, edited by Joanne M. Braxton and Andree Nicola McLaughlin and *Southern Women Writers: The New Generation*, edited by Tonette Bond Inge. Her articles have also appeared in *The Dictionary of Literary Biography*, *The Zora Neale Hurston Forum*, *The Oxford Companion to Women's Writing*, the *Langston Hughes Journal*, *Callaloo*, *The Oxford Companion to African American Literature*, and *Black Books Bulletin*.

A dedicated teacher and scholar, she has received forty awards for excellence in teaching, scholarship and leadership. Among them are the College Language Association Creative Scholarship Award for her book *Sterling A. Brown* (1986), the James Madison University Faculty Women's Caucus and Women's Resource Network Award for Scholarship (1988), the Outstanding Faculty Award, Virginia State Council of Higher Education (1993), and the Provost Award for Excellence (2004).

SAM GREENLEE is a novelist, poet, playwright, screenwriter, producer, director, journalist, teacher, former tract star, and an actor. Mr. Greenlee is author of the award-winning book, *The Spook Who Sat by the Door* (1969). Awards include the *London Sunday Times* Book of the Year Award (1969) and the *Ebony* Magazine Ten Best Black Films of All Times Award (1988, 1993). The *Spook Who Sat by the Door* was translated into German, Italian, Swedish, Finnish, Dutch, and Japanese. Mr. Greenlee is also author of the novel entitled *Baghdad Blues* (1976). His volumes of poems include *Blues for an African Princess* (1970), *Ammunition: Poetry and Other Raps* (1976), and *Be-Bop Ma/ Be-Bop Woman* (1995). Mr. Greenlee earned a Bachelor of Science degree at University of Wisconsin and completed postgraduate work at University of Chicago and University of Thessaloniki in Greece. Awards include the Meritorious Service Award for his work as a U.S. Information Agency Foreign Service Officer in Iraq, Pakistan, Indonesia, and Greece.

QURAYSH ALI LANSANA is author of three poetry books, including *They Shall Run: Harriet Tubman Poems* (Third World Press, 2004) a children's book, and editor of five anthologies. He is Director of the Gwendolyn Brooks Center for Black Literature and Creative Writing at Chicago State University, where he is also an assistant professor of English and Creative Writing. Quraysh serves as Associate Editor-Poetry for *Black Issues Book Review*, and sits on the Editorial Board of Tia Chucha Press. Quraysh earned a Masters of Fine Arts degree at the Creative Writing Program at New York University, where he was a Departmental Fellow.

PAULE MARSHALL is a novelist, short fiction writer, lecturer, professor, and an essayist. She is author of five novels: *Brown Girl, Brownstones* (1959), *The Chosen Place, the Timeless People* (1969), *Praisesong for the Widow* (1983), *Daughters* (1991), and *The Fisher King* (2000). She has also published two collections of short fiction, *Soul Clap Hands and Sing* (1961) and *Reena and Other Stories* (1983). Paule Marshall has received numerous awards, including the Rosenthal Award from the National Institute of Arts and Letters, a Guggenheim Fellowship, a Mac Arthur Fellowship, and grants from the Ford Foundation and the National Endowment for the Arts. She is also a past winner of the Dos Passos Prize for Literature. Paule Marshall has taught at University of California at Berkeley, Yale University, Virginia Commonwealth University, and the Iowa Writers Workshop. She currently holds a distinguished Chair in Creative Writing at New York University.

D. H. MELHEM is the author of *Gwendolyn Brooks: Poetry and the Heroic Voice* (University Press of Kentucky), the first comprehensive study of the poet. Brooks is one of six subjects in Dr. Melhem's American Book Award-winning *Heroism in the New Black Poetry: Introductions and Interviews* (also from Kentucky). A poet herself, her seventh collection, *New York Poems*, was just published by Syracuse University Press (2005), which also distributes her novel *Blight*. She edited two anthologies, had her musical drama produced in New York, wrote a creative writing book, and published over 60 essays. Known internationally, Dr. Melhem conducted a poetry workshop in October 2005 in Geneva, Switzerland.

GWENDOLYN A. MITCHELL is a poet and an editor. Her poetry has appeared in a number of journals and anthologies including *American Review*, *Prairie Schooner*, *WarpLand: A Journal of Black Literature and Ideas*, and *Essence Magazine*. She has conducted workshops in writing and literary arts, and in 2000, served as the first poet-in-residence for the Tougaloo Art Colony. She received her Master of Fine Arts in English from Pennsylvania State University. Ms. Mitchell is the author of *Veins and Rivers* and *House of Women*. She is the co-editor of two anthologies, *Releasing the Spirit* and *Describe the Moment*, both collections of literary work from Gallery 37 in Chicago. Gwendolyn Mitchell resides in Illinois, where she serves as Senior Editor for Third World Press.

GEORGENE BESS MONTGOMERY received her Ph.D in English from the University of Maryland, College Park. Her dissertation "Ifa as a Paradigm for the Interpretation of African American and Caribbean Literature" utililzes Ifa, an ancient African spiritual system, to create a paradigm for examining and decoding African American and Caribbean literary texts. She is an assistant professor in the Department of English at Clark Atlanta University. Dr. Montgomery has one daughter, Zora Indigo Montgomery.

ADELE NEWSON-HORST is Dean, College of Arts and Letters at Missouri State University and Professor of English. Dr. Newson-Horst has written review essays for *World Literature Today* for more than ten years and specializes in African American, Caribbean, and African literatures. In addition to a reference guide on Zora Neale Hurston (G.K. Hall 1988), she has also published *Winds of Change: The Transforming Voices of Caribbean Women Writers and Scholars* (with Linda Strong-Leek, 1998, Peter Lang). Other works include the chapters "Maud Martha Brown: A Study in Emergence" (2002) and "Zee Edgell's Birth of Belize" (1999). She is currently writing on the Privilege Class Tradition in African American Literature.

MWATABU OKANTAH holds the BA degree in English and African Studies from Kent State University (1976) and the MA in Creative Writing from the City College of New York (1982). Currently, he is an assistant professor and a Poet in Residence in the Department of Pan-African Studies at Kent State University. He also serves as Director of the Center of Pan-African Culture. As a poet, performer and motivational speaker, Mr. Okantah has appeared throughout the USA, Canada and West Africa. He has worked as Griot for the Iroko African Drum & Dance Society and in an ongoing collaboration with the Cavani String Quartet. Presently, he is the leader of the Muntu Kuntu Energy Ensemble-a four piece performance group. Honors include Selection to the 5th Edition of *Who's Who Among Teachers in America*, inclusion in the *International Who's Who in Poetry*, and selection in *Outstanding Writers of the 20th Century* by the International Biographical Centre. In 1994, Okantah served as a "special guest" guide for Sankofa Tours in Senegal and Ghana. In 1988, he was named a Rotary International Group Study Exchange Fellow in Nigeria. Mr. Okantah has also taught at Union College, The Livingston College of Rutgers University, Cleveland State University, and Lakeland Community College. He is the author of *Afreeka Brass* (1983), *Collage* (1984), and *Cheikh Anta Diop: Poem for the Living* (1997), published as a limited trilingual edition in English, French and Wolof. Work has been anthologized in *Why L. A. Happened* (1993),

Soul Looks Back In Wonder (1994), *The Second Set Vol. 2* (1996), *Warpland* (1999), *Journey to TimBookTu* (2001), and *Beyond the Frontier: African-American Poetry for the 21st Century* (2002). A Spoken Word & Original Music CD, *Guerrilla Dread: Griot Stylee*, was released in 2005. Published by Africa World Press, Mr. Okantah's most recent work is *Reconnecting Memories: Dreams No Longer Deferred* (2004).

USENI EUGENE PERKINS has worked with Black youth for over forty-five years in many capacities. He directed a gang outreach program at the Henry Horner Boys Club, served as director of the Better Boys Foundation, President of the Urban League of Portland, Oregon and, recently, director the Family Life Center at Chicago State University. In addition, he is the president of the Association for the Positive Development of Black Youth and has been recognized as one of the pioneers of the Rites of Passage Movement. In 2002, he organized the first Community Outreach Conference held at the St. Charles Juvenile Correctional Center. Mr. Perkins is also nationally recognized for his writing on youth. Lerone Bennett, Jr., cited his book, *Home is a Dirty Street: The Social Oppression of Black Children* as one of the most important books on the sociology of the streets since the publication of *Black Metropolis*. Other books by Mr. Perkins include *Harvesting New Generations: The Positive Development of Black Youth*, *Explosion of Chicago's Black Street Gangs: 1970 to Present*, and the *Afrocentric Self-Discovery Workbook for Black Youth*. Mr. Perkins was editor and publisher of *Black Child Journal* and editor of *Successful Black Parenting Magazine*. Other publications include seven volumes of poetry which include *An Apology To My African Brother*, *Silhouette*, *Black is Beautiful*, *Midnight Blues in the Afternoon*, and *Memories and Images: Selected Poems*, Third

World Press (2002). He has published numerous articles in professional journals and anthologies. Mr. Perkins teaches playwriting in the MFA program at Chicago State University.

L. E. SCOTT, African American writer and jazz poet, was born in Arabi, Georgia (USA).

Mr. Scott is constantly experimenting with the sounds and cadences of the spoken word of the Black Church, which underpins the essence of his work. He defines his work as jazz blues, a repetition of sound that he trusts much more than the creation of defined words. The sound is a human tongue drum licking the flesh, sticking deeply in your ears to suck the taste of your mind and leaving in your consciousness the agony of a stolen race from Africa.

Mr. Scott's work has been published in magazines, newspapers, journals and anthologies in the USA, New Zealand, and Australia. He has also had 15 books of poetry and prose published, dealing with subjects ranging from his childhood in the American South of the 1950s, to his experience in the Vietnam War and his involvement in the civil rights struggle in the 1960s and 1970s, to the universality of the human condition.

DOROTHY RANDALL TSURUTA is chair of Africana Studies at San Francisco State University (SFSU) and serves there as editor/advisor to the renowned *SFSU Black Studies Journal*. She also served as consultant and contributor to *Call and Response, The Riverside Anthology of the African American Literary Tradition* (Houghton and Mifflin, 1998). While a graduate student, as a Kellogg Fellow, she participated on a Fulbright team, traveling and studying in Senegal, Nigeria, and Ghana, in the latter focusing her study on the role of

Ashanti women in the military. Recent publications appeared in *Gwendolyn Brooks' Maud Martha: A Critical Collection* (Third World Press, 2002); *Concerns: A Publication of the Women's Caucus of the Modern Language Association* (Spring 2002), and *Sasongo The Cameron Review of the Arts* (June 2000). Her poetry has appeared in the *Black Scholar*, *The Black Studies Journal*, and *Best of Show* (Detroit Writers' Guild, 2002) having placed among the winners in the Paul Lawrence Dunbar Poetry Contest. Among her works in progress are *A Black Cannon: Rev. Elmer Augustus McLaughlin* 1989-1994; and *Off Campus to Lunch*; In addition are her creative works in progress.

SHIRLEY N. WEBER is an associate professor and chair of the Department of Africana Studies at San Diego State University. She is the past President of the National Council for Black Studies. Her areas of specialization are Black Nationalism, Garveyism and Black Language. Her articles have been published in *Journal of Black Studies* and *Western Journal of Black Studies*, and she has chapters in several books on black studies, education, culture and language. As the former president of the San Diego City School Board of Education, she is co-director of the Academy for Professional Development that retrains teachers on Effectively Teaching African American Students. She conducts study abroad programs and service learning projects in Ghana and South Africa.

EDITOR

JACQUELINE IMANI BRYANT is a professor of English and an affiliate faculty member of African American Studies at Chicago State University. Her works appear in *Journal of Black Studies, CLA Journal, WarpLand: A Journal of Black Literature and Ideas, A Jubilee Project of Olivet Institutional Baptist Church* (Editor, The Reverend Dr. Otis Moss, Jr., Fairway Press, 2002), and *African American Rhetoric*(s) (Editors, Elaine B. Richardson and Ronald L. Jackson, Southern Illinois University Press, 2004). Other works include the book, *The Foremother Figure in Early Black Women's Literature*: "*Clothed in My Right Mind,*"(Garland Publishing,1999) and *Gwendolyn Brooks' Maud Martha: A Critical Collection*, (Editor, Jacqueline Bryant, Third World Press, 2002).

PERMISSIONS